Wait a Hot Minute!

How to Manage Your Life with the Minutes You Have

Jacquelyn Gaines, MS, RN

Published by:
Fire Starter Publishing
350 West Cedar Street
Suite 300
Pensacola, FL 32502
Phone: 866-354-3473
Fax: 850-332-5117
www.firestarterpublishing.com

ISBN: 978-1-6221805-4-7

Library of Congress Control Number: 2016941732

The stories in this book are true. However, names and identifying details have been changed to protect the privacy of all concerned.

Printed in the United States of America

This book is dedicated to my dad, Herbert Van Keyes, who passed away at the end of 2014. It was in his passing that I realized the importance of each minute in my life. Each minute should be cherished as quality time for yourself and all you love.

Table of Contents

How Did We Arrive in This Place?

"The bad news is time flies. The good news is you're the pilot."

—Michael Altahuler

It's 5:00 a.m. I have been trying to go back to sleep for the last two hours, but my mind is flooded with thoughts and images of all the things I need to accomplish over the next week: projects to finalize at work, vacation planning, writing an article, my grandson's football games this weekend, a hair appointment, doctor's appointment, preparing for that upcoming lecture, household chores (never-ending!), Zumba, and spending quality time with my husband...the list goes on (and on).

As I slowly realize that sleep isn't going to happen, it becomes clear that my mind is attempting to sort my priorities for the day...all on its own! When did my life get so complicated? When did my to-do list become so long? I am already trying to multitask in my head before I even leave the warmth of my bed. I think I need a wake-up call!

Once I arise and grab a cup of coffee, the madness really begins—e-mails, morning news, and breakfast all at the same time. I want to get as much done as I can before my husband awakens, so I can have a decent conversation with him to start the day. By 6:30 a.m., I am tired enough for a nap! Good grief. No time. I need to stay focused, complete prep for my first conference call of the day, get dressed, and call my mom to check on her. I yearn for the "old days" when multitasking was not so much a part of my life.

Does this scenario sound familiar? I would guess that my morning madness resonates with many people who find their lives increasingly complex and full of competing priorities. Some feel completely out of control and choose to multitask as a solution to better manage their time, even though they would readily admit that multitasking is not a great choice.

And current generations did not invent multitasking or the need for time management. Multitasking is actually inherent in all of us, dating all the way back to prehistoric times. In an interview with *UCLA Newsroom*, Monica L. Smith, the author of *A Prehistory of Ordinary People*, states:

"Once man started walking on two feet, their hands were free to pick up tools, fibers, fruits, or kids, and their eyes could look around for opportunities and dangers," she said. "That's the beginning of multitasking right there. By the time tool-making started 1.5 million years ago, the ability to multitask would have been essential because the linear sequence of tool production would have been subject to frequent interruptions. Great deeds have been made possible by the collective experience of people who multitasked through their everyday lives…and then who devoted some extra portion of their time, energy, and the fruits of their labor into coming up

with fabulous inventions and building complex societies. Yet in the popular imagination, contemporary times have some kind of corner on the multi-tasking market. People seem to think that the past was this simpler time with fewer interruptions because so many of the modern gadgets we have today had yet to be invented. But we've been multitasking from the beginning. Every object that we have from the past is the result of a dynamic process where people were being interrupted all the time."[1]

So you can see that multitasking is not really "bad"—after all, a certain amount of it is inevitable—but I would suggest that the frantic tangle of trying to get everything done at once is not the best way to live (and enjoy) our lives. We've been struggling to better manage our minutes since the dawn of time, and all these years later, not much has changed. Though we have all the conveniences of modern life, the minutes making up our day have stayed the same over the years: 1,440 hot minutes with which to order our lives in an efficient and well-organized manner.

At least our ancestors didn't have to handle the disruptions caused by today's technology! Sitting in the doctor's office recently, I had an out-of-body experience. There I was in a waiting room full of people. I lifted my eyes from my magazine and became overwhelmed by the acute awareness of what was going on around me. Most of my fellow patients had their heads bowed in deference to their "I"s. You know—their phones, tablets, and anything else connecting them to the Internet and giving them the all-too-important distraction that they craved. Some were making calls for work and scheduling appointments.

I could actually feel the hustle and bustle of their multitasking activities even though the room was still and quiet. I sensed that the "noise" of all this distraction was drowning out the emotions and thoughts that connected these people to their lives. **Wait a hot minute!** When did distraction and multitasking become the new "normal"?

Few people today ever hit the pause button long enough to really *be* in the moment in their personal or professional lives. The constant *connection* to the Internet has become an addiction that draws us in and hooks us like a powerful drug. Some of us even listen for the incessant "bing" of our phones as we try to sleep. This addiction can blur the lines between work and play and even strain the healthiest relationships.

Think about it. When we are constantly in "mental motion," we lose a little of ourselves in the madness. Our thoughts seem to move from one subject to the next without pause in a matter of minutes—or sometimes seconds. And the powerful "I" isn't the only way that we squander our precious time. As I sat and pondered my observations, I wondered how much of myself I had lost or given away to all the *distractions* and *time robbers* in my own life.

I became determined then and there to change what I could to regain a bit of me—one "hot minute" at a time. I want to help you make this shift, too.

Often, we may feel that we cannot control many aspects of our lives. This is particularly true of our time spent at work. We serve at the mercy of our employers who can directly and indirectly impact how we spend our work minutes each day. But, is it *really* true that we have no control over our work minutes? Are there ways we can minimize wasted time?

Whether time is a challenge for you in your personal life, professional life, or both, the information in this book can help you regain some of your lost minutes. Still, this is not just another book about time management, but one about managing your life in the context of the time you have. Gaining more conscious and mindful control of how we spend our time is the closest we can possibly come to slowing the relentless flow of the sand through the hourglass.

I hope you'll take a hot minute out of your busy day and join me on this journey. We all need to learn how to slow down, breathe deeply, and enjoy the riches life puts in our path (if only we take the time to see them!). If this book can help guide your steps in some small way, I will be honored.

CHAPTER ONE:

The Time Machine

> *"We are always getting away from the present moment. Our mental existence, which are immaterial and have no dimensions, are passing along the Time-Dimension with a uniform velocity from the cradle to the grave."*
> —H.G. Wells

If only I had another couple hours! Better yet, does this day have a restart button? There are moments in our lives when we all wish we could be time travelers—when we would give just about anything to have a "do-over," or at least fast forward to a time that gives us the opportunity to breathe. Once reality sets back in and we realize that time machines don't exist, we have to accept that we are stuck in the here and now, with the 24 hours we've been given.

Let's take a look at our complicated relationship with the one-way "time machine" that is our lives. Where does our time go? Why do we always wish we had more of it? How much is it *actually* possible for us to accomplish each day?

Why Don't We Have More Time?

Indoor plumbing, electric stoves, washing machines, clothes dryers, computers, and even the telephone were all created to make our lives easier and to save us time. No longer do we have to gather wood to cook a meal or spend all afternoon scrubbing our clothes in a bin. The computer replaced the typewriter, and now we can stay connected through our phones 24 hours a day. Just think of all those hot minutes saved to improve the quality of our lives. We should be getting so much relief from all these inventions our forefathers and foremothers gifted to us, right? Unfortunately, it's just the opposite. We're busier than ever. *What happened?*

Is there really more on our to-do lists, or has the ongoing cultural shift toward instant gratification just made it seem that way? Are we losing our patience with a slower pace of existence (even though speed doesn't always guarantee quality of life or emotional well-being)? And do social economics make a difference in how we use our time?

I think it's clear that new technologies like e-mail and smartphones have made us more impatient (and in many cases, more anxious). E-mail etiquette often necessitates a response within 24 hours, with the general understanding that sooner is better. Managing this constant and mounting demand often involves switching tasks or multitasking, and the job never quite feels done.

Shifts in the way people work and live have also changed the way leisure time is experienced and who gets to experience it. Years ago, low-paid blue-collar workers were more likely to punch in a long day than their professional counterparts. One of the many perks of being a salaried employee was a fairly manageable and predictable workweek. The workday had a definite beginning and end.

Today, the tables have been turned. Many professionals are working the longest hours of all. Lunches tend to be efficient affairs, devoured at one's desk, with an eye on the e-mail in-box. At some point these employees may finally leave the office, but the regular blinking or chirping of their smartphones kindly serves to remind them that their work is never done. In other words, since there is no set "quitting time," the line between work and play has become very blurred. So yes, I think, in many instances there *are* more items on our to-do lists, and we are socially and professionally pressured to complete them more quickly than we might have been in the past.

Writing in the first century, Roman philosopher and author Seneca was startled by how little people seemed to value their lives as they were living them. He lamented how terribly busy everyone seemed to be, as well as how wasteful they were of their time. He noticed how even wealthy people hustled their lives along as they built their fortunes, always anticipating a time in the future when they would rest.

"People are frugal in guarding their personal property; but as soon as it comes to squandering time they are most wasteful of the one thing in which it is right to be stingy," he observed in *On the Shortness of Life*, perhaps the very first time-management self-help book. "Time on Earth may be uncertain and fleeting, but nearly everyone has enough of it to take some deep breaths, think deep thoughts and smell some roses, deeply. Life is long if you know how to use it," he counselled.[1] We could all grow personally and professionally from his words today.

> *"Don't say you don't have enough time. You have exactly the same number of hours per day that were given to Helen Keller, Pasteur, Michelangelo, Mother Teresa, Leonardo da Vinci, Thomas Jefferson, and Albert Einstein."*
>
> —H. Jackson Brown, Jr.

24 Hours Is Still 24 Hours

> *"If one advances confidently in the direction of his dreams, and endeavors to live the life which he has imagined, he will meet with a success unexpected in common hours."*
>
> —Henry David Thoreau

If someone were to ask, "Can you *live* comfortably within the confines of a 24-hour day?" How would you respond? I believe most people would answer with a resounding "no." The reality is that few of us want to make the sacrifices needed to live comfortably within a 24-hour period. Nor do we want to make those tough choices that would help decrease stress and anxiety in our lives. Yet, the personal and professional commitment to improving your quality of life and maximizing your time on this Earth is totally in your hands. It is a never-ending discipline with an incredible end result that will benefit not only you but others around you as well.

When we are not running around trying to squeeze 36 hours into 24 hours, the quality of our relationships changes, we become happier, and we are able to accomplish much more than we would otherwise. Effectively managing our schedules within the 24-hour timeframe can also sharpen our focus and help us accomplish our daily tasks with precision.

Trust me, that same mountain of tasks and projects cluttering up your to-do list will still be there waiting for you tomorrow (and the day after that!). The "cramming" technique of squeezing in too much activity results in an understandable lack of focus, silly mistakes, and sheer exhaustion. It actually *prolongs* your time commitments rather than shortening them, whereas the act of *pacing* your tasks ensures that you stay rested and focused. In time, this technique may dramatically reduce the amount of work you need to redo, which further bolsters your productivity.

Another consideration is how we define "a day." Even though the number of hours in a day has not changed since the dawn of time, our perception of "a day" can vary depending on the context. For example, there are workdays, weekend days, vacation days, sick days, and holidays. Even though you didn't personally assign value or any specific expectation to any of these given days, you are no doubt influenced by the value and importance of them.

Imagine that you have taken a job with an organization whose values resonate with your own. The job promotes work/life balance, with the written expectation that you work 40 hours per week. This balance is very important to you because you still have young children at home and quality time before and after work is a personal priority. Yet, once you start working, you realize that you are actually expected to work more than the previously agreed upon 40 hours. The *actual* norm is more like 50 hours per week—plus the expectation that you answer e-mails and phone calls during family time.

Clearly the definitions of a "workday" are not the same for you as they are for your employer. Now you have to make a choice: Either fall in line with your employer's norm and surrender the priorities that allow you a *comfortable life* or confront your boss about your needs and be willing to walk away if they are not met. As this scenario shows, you will no doubt encounter others whose perception of "a day" differs from your own.

Vacations and holidays seem to present a whole different concept of time as well. Take Christmas in my house for instance. Traditionally, everyone spends the night together on Christmas Eve and wakes up early to the sounds of the children in the house eager to see what Santa left under the tree. The noise usually starts at 5:00 a.m. and doesn't stop until we are all awake. The day is all about joy and love. There is no pressure to get things done, no to-do lists, just us, living in the moment.

I can close my eyes and still see those precious times when my adult children were those little ones at our bedroom door. Those images bring me joy. Wow, what if all the images of how we spend our time had the same effect?

Have you noticed that when we really enjoy what we are doing, time seems to fly? Yet, when we are stressed or are doing something that conflicts with our values or priorities, the clock stops. Still, it's the same 24 hours, right? Of course it is!

Here's another question: Does *sleep time* "count"? If you're like me, you may sometimes feel that the eight (or seven or six or maybe even fewer!) hours you spend between the sheets goes by in five minutes. Yet sleep absolutely does count—by which I mean we need to pay attention to how much we're sleeping and how restful that sleep is.

After all, the amount of sleep we get directly influences the amount of time we have out of 24 hours for everything else—not to mention our alertness and energy to *do* anything else. Most of us know that getting a good night's sleep is important, but too few of us actually make those eight or so hours between the sheets a priority. To further complicate matters, stimulants like coffee and energy drinks, alarm clocks, and external lights—including those from electronic devices—interfere with our natural sleeping and waking cycle.

Getting a good night's sleep must move up on your priority list. Even though research varies on exactly how much sleep people actually need, we all know how a lack of sleep makes us feel. Self-assess how different levels of sleep affect you. You should aim for however many hours you need in order to achieve peak performance (mentally and physically). And let's be realistic, fewer than five hours is not the right answer.

Some research studies have shown that when workers slept for fewer than five hours before work or when workers were awake for more than 16 hours, their chance of making mistakes at work due to fatigue increased significantly.

Research studies have shown that the more hours participants spend awake, the more their behavior mimics the effects of higher blood alcohol levels. The Canadian Centre for Occupational Health and Safety reports the following:

- 17 hours awake is equivalent to a blood alcohol content of 0.05

- 21 hours awake is equivalent to a blood alcohol content of 0.08 (legal limit in Canada)

- 24-25 hours awake is equivalent to a blood alcohol content of .10

In addition, they list the following as the potential effects of fatigue or lack of sleep:

- Reduced decision making ability

- Reduced ability to do complex planning

- Reduced communication skills

- Reduced productivity/performance

- Reduced attention and vigilance

- Reduced ability to handle stress on the job

- Reduced reaction time—both in speed and thought

- Loss of memory or the ability to recall details

- Failure to respond to changes in surroundings or information provided

- Unable to stay awake (e.g., falling asleep while operating machinery or driving a vehicle)

- Increased tendency for risk taking

- Increased forgetfulness

- Increased errors in judgment

- Increased sick time, absenteeism, rate of turnover

- Increased medical costs
- Increased accident rates[2]

And sleep isn't the only "obligatory" task. Let's not forget the time that is needed for those other needs essential to life… like proper meal times and self-care. How often do these key tasks get relegated to the "only if I have time category" or are completed in conjunction with another task? In a quick survey of colleagues and friends, I asked them to describe their multitasking bad habits. The following list reflects their responses. Do any of these resonate with your current lifestyle?

- Eating in the car or while driving (most likely less-than-nutritious fast food!)
- Talking on the phone while driving
- Taking the phone into the bathroom
- Checking e-mail on the run or during conference calls (for fear of missing something)
- Eating while making the kids' lunches
- Surfing the web or playing video games while talking to family or friends
- Working on more than one project at a time (and getting confused about what needs to be done for which project)

* SIDENOTE: It's no coincidence that the majority of the responses in the quick survey related to some form of electronics as the major distraction.

Even our meal times have been invaded so that work can continue. Indeed, the working breakfast, lunch, or dinner is now the norm. This allows us virtually no down time to catch our breath, take care of personal needs, or mentally recharge for the rest of the day. How many of us even taste our food or remember what we ate (unless it offers us the gift of indigestion)? How many of these working meetings have you reluctantly participated in? Do they really add value to the work if people are not fully engaged or at their best?

When we consider the 24-hour day, why are personal tasks deemed unimportant in the scope of things when they are essential to our very survival? I believe we all grapple with the false belief that our accomplishments are somehow more important than our quality of life. We simply need to overcome the kneejerk urge to put ourselves last. Everyone not only needs but deserves adequate rest, family time, relaxing meals, and even leisure time. When you allow yourself these momentous yet attainable gifts, your life once again becomes livable—even joyous. And a joyous life is what it's all about.

The Human Potential

"Some days, 24 hours is too much to stay put in, so I take the day hour by hour, moment by moment. I break the task, the challenge, the fear into small, bite-size pieces. I can handle a piece of fear, depression, anger, pain, sadness, loneliness, illness. I actually put my hands up to my face, one next to each eye, like blinders on a horse."

—Regina Brett

We have all heard that there is only so much you can get done in a day. So how do you know when you have exceeded *your* limit for what is possible in 24 hours? You'll know when you feel as if you are about to implode because your life seems completely out of control. You'll know when time seems to be a rare commodity on both personal and professional levels.

I once relocated across the country to take on the role of CEO for an organization. The stress of relocating alone can push almost anyone over the edge. Closing out one job, farewell parties from family and friends, selling your old house and buying a new house, packing and unpacking, getting personal business affairs in order, meeting new staff, welcoming parties, board meetings, starting the new job: These are just a few of the items on my relocation to-do list. I am a very organized person, so many of these tasks were written on a checklist I kept on my nightstand.

What the list did not include, however, were the other priorities impacting how I spent my time each day and my sanity. Things like quality time with my family (who were having emotional issues dealing with the relocation), eating and sleeping, and the time to just breathe. I felt I needed to focus more on getting all my tasks done and less on the things I needed to sustain my mental, physical, and emotional well-being. There were just not enough hours in a day. If one more person asked me to do something, I knew I would implode.

Yet I didn't implode. Somehow, my capacity for doing *more* exceeded even my expectations. Somehow, I crammed more into those 24 hours, but at what expense to my health and quality of life? Thankfully, this was a very small window of time. The problem comes when we try to live like this all the time. The issue is not that we can't do more, but whether doing more is always a wise choice. The real question is, "What am I willing to sacrifice if I take on more?" Sadly, it's often the personal side of our lives.

There is also the question of our mental capacity to do more. In a *Fast Company* article titled "The Exact Amount of Time You Should Work Every Day," the author, Lisa Evans, argues that our brains have a limited pool of psychological energy. She states, "All efforts to control behavior, to perform, and to focus draw on that pool of psychological energy. Once that energy source is depleted, we become less effective at everything that we do." Our brains simply weren't built to focus for eight full hours a day. The best way to refresh your focus is to step away and take a break.[3]

A current trend in the workplace is the extended workday (working 12- to 16-hour days in exchange for more "free" days). A primary advantage of the extended workday is that it provides more consecutive days off than most other types of schedules. This allows more free days for family and other activities. However, the disadvantage is that the long hours do not allow much free time on workdays. This can also affect family and social life. Whether the advantage of longer blocks of time off outweighs the disadvantage of little time off on workdays, or vice versa, may depend on the individual.

But the extended workdays model is not right for everyone. An important factor for being able to adjust to an extended workday more than likely relates to characteristics such as age, marital status, parental status, hobbies, and personal interests. People who have major responsibilities outside work may have more difficulty with conflicting demands for time on extended workdays—particularly during the 12-hour day. On the other hand, others may enjoy the longer time off and the opportunity for social and leisure activities.

Time spent traveling to and from work is often viewed as lost time. The extended workday structure means fewer commuting trips and, therefore, less wasted time and less cost.

An additional consideration in choosing an extended workday is the actual expectations of the job, including its physical, mental, and emotional demands. For example, work that requires constant attention or intense mental effort may be less appropriate for the extended workday and may require additional breaks. Furthermore, work that requires prolonged physical exertion may not even be possible for Hercules, much less regular people.

Many of us use the expression "My plate is too full" to describe when we have reached our maximum capacity of busyness. I have heard this phrase used throughout my career, often by the same people. I have come to the conclusion that we never really empty our plates; we just move the food around. Some of us heap on additional portions, never taking anything off. And we moan and groan about the personal burden of our heavy plate, when portion control is in our hands all along.

It's as if we are going through life's buffet line and we just can't help ourselves, taking on more and more when we know we don't need it. We know we will regret it later and yet we can't seem to stop ourselves. In the workplace and in our personal life, we say "yes" to our friends and colleagues, when we know we need rest. The common themes in all this are *choice* and *sacrifice*. It's not so much that our plate is too full, but rather our ability to eat in moderation is out of control.

"We all create the person we become by our choices as we go through life. In a real sense, by the time we are adults, we are the sum total of the choices we have made."
—Eleanor Roosevelt

The Powerful "I"

"We are all now connected by the Internet, like neurons in a giant brain."
—Stephen Hawking

Ahhh, 7:00 p.m. arrives and I am finally able to lean back in my blue easy chair to relax after a long workday. Another

Law and Order episode is on my TV screen looking at me as I put my feet up on the ottoman. Once settled, I arrange my toys for easy access. You know, my iPhones (two of them: work and personal) and iPad so I can access the Internet until I go upstairs for bed. Like a warped symphony, these toys bing, buzz, tic, and serenade me until I respond. And, with the precision of a musician, I do—stroking and tapping the keyboards and screens effortlessly. My focus is intense, overpowering the words coming out of my husband's mouth about his day. I mumble back to him, but keep my eyes locked on the "I." The world may actually stop if I look away.

Rewind to the day prior when I visited my daughter and grandchildren. My oldest grandson is 11 years old and is completely hooked on video games. I really wanted to spend time with him, but getting him to surface from the game room even for a quick kiss was a monumental feat. I yearned for the old days when he would snuggle with me on the sofa or let me read to him. When did video basketball replace the real thing?

When did technology take over our lives to the point of disruption? And, when did I get myself lost in the madness?

New gadgets seem to appear daily with the promise of making our lives easier and saving us time. Dr. David Greenfield, in his blog "Virtual Addiction: Sometimes New Technology Can Create New Problems," states:

Technology, and most especially, computers and the Internet, seem to be at best easily overused/abused, and at worst, addictive. The combination of available stimulating content, ease of access, convenience, low cost, visual stimulation, autonomy, and anonymity—all contribute to a highly psychoactive experience. By psychoactive, that is to say mood altering, and potentially behaviorally impactful. In other words these technologies affect the manner in which we live and love. It is my contention that some of these effects are indeed less than positive, and may contribute to various negative psychological effects.

Even seemingly innocuous advances such as the elevator, remote controls, credit card gas pumps, dishwashers, and drive-through everything, all have unintended negative effects. They all save time and energy, but the energy they save may prevent us from using our physical bodies as they were designed to be used. In short we have convenienced ourselves to a sedentary lifestyle.[4]

We feel the overwhelming need to stay "connected" just because we can! In the *good old days* we picked up the phone to talk to our family and friends or maybe we even went to see them. Now we text and e-mail.

There is a commercial currently on TV that demonstrates just how "over the edge" we are with our use of technology. Two sisters sit on either side of their dad on the living room sofa. Both have their phones in their hands and are texting each other. The dad cannot believe what he is witnessing! Even though this commercial is intended to be lighthearted, it absolutely reflects our current state of communication. Think about your own behavior. How readily do you text or e-mail? How have your relationships changed as a result?

On the surface, technology, like iPhones, appears to be a great time saver, but it causes you to spend more time trying to fix the miscommunications inherent in using written words or the cryptic language of texting. A real human-to-human connection adds tone and texture to the discussion. Add face time (whether over video chat or in person) and you have non-verbal cues that help tell a complete story. There is also a higher probability that you will have a single focus in a face-to-face discussion and not get drawn into the multitasking cycle (no guarantees here, but a better shot at success).

The Internet may offer a vast amount of information and social interaction that stimulates our intellect and imagination. But it will never replace the benefits of human-to-human interaction. The necessary forms of social and emotional intelligence that we need in order to ensure healthy relationships may be lacking in cyber-communications. When you spend too much time online, you are not doing other things that create a well-balanced life. That is not to say that the Internet is a bad place, nor is it to say that we cannot utilize its vast resources. But there is a huge difference between using the Internet wisely and getting lost in cyberspace.

Speaking of technology, just how much time *do* we spend interacting with our toys? According to Nielsen's Total Audience Report, Americans aged 18 and older spend more than 11 hours a day watching TV, listening to the radio, or using smartphones and other electronic devices.[5] If most of us are awake 16-18 hours a day, and such a huge chunk of that time is taken up by electronic devices, multitasking seems inevitable. Ugh!

In their book, *Internet Addiction: A Handbook and Guide to Evaluation and Treatment*, Kimberly Young and Cristiano Nabuco de Abreu describe virtual addiction as having "persistent desire, tolerance, withdrawal, negative consequences."[6] The Center for Internet and Technology Addiction's Virtual Addiction Test is used in determining overuse versus addiction requiring clinical support to detach.

- Do you feel "out of control" when using the Internet or cell phones (i.e., feeling "carried away")?

- When not on the Internet, do you find that you are preoccupied with the Internet, computers, or cell phones (e.g., thinking about or reliving past experiences on the

Internet, planning your next experience on the Internet, or thinking of ways to gain access to the Internet in the future)?

- Do you find that you need to spend greater amounts of time on the Internet to achieve satisfaction similar to previous events?

- Have you had repeated, unsuccessful efforts to control, cut back, or stop using the Internet or detach from your cell phone?

- Do you find yourself to be restless or irritable when attempting to cut down or stop using the Internet or limit how many times you check your phone?

- Are you using the Internet as a way of escaping from problems or relieving a bad mood (e.g., feelings of helplessness, guilt, anxiety, or depression)?

- After spending what you consider an excessive amount of time on the Internet and vowing not to do so the next day, do you find yourself back on the next day or soon after?

- Do you find yourself lying to family members, therapists, or others to conceal the extent of your involvement with the Internet?

- Have you jeopardized or lost a significant relationship, job, or educational or career opportunity because of your use of the Internet?[7]

Reality check: Did you answer yes to any of these?

> *"The Internet is so big, so powerful and pointless that for some people it is a complete substitute for life."*
>
> —Andrew Brown

Generational Differences

> *"The greatest discovery of my generation is that human beings can alter their lives by altering their attitudes of mind. As you think, so shall you be."*
>
> —William James

As a grandmother of three and mother of two grown daughters, I have the opportunity to see the world through the lens of multiple generations. None of those generations seem to mirror the planet that my husband and I reside on. We all couldn't be more different! This seems to be particularly true as it relates to this concept of time. What my husband and I value in each moment the new day brings varies widely from the values of my kids and grandkids.

I, for example, am up early, relishing the quiet of the morning before phones begin to ring or conversation ensues. I love to just "be" in the morning minutes that belong to just me. Sometimes those precious minutes are for boot camp to keep me healthy, sometimes I am writing or catching up on reading, and sometimes I just do nothing and that's okay too.

For my children (all of them!) sleeping "in" as long as they can is the order of the day. I can call my mother who is 81 years old and up like me by 7:00 a.m., but I dare not call my children until after 9:00 a.m. Even then, I get a groggy hello. They are constantly talking about and planning their next vacation while I am thinking, *How will I ever be able to take time off with all the work I have in front of me?* I am positive that work anxiety doesn't wake them up from *their* sleep.

And, don't get me started on how much time it takes younger generations to complete a task. If I hear "in a minute" one more time, I may explode. My minutes actually mean minutes. Their minutes mean *when I can fit it in* or *if I remember to do it at all.* This is definitely evidence of the generational difference between us (I'm a Baby Boomer). When my parents asked me to do something, I moved immediately.

Maybe these new dynamics have developed because fear was once a motivating factor in the parent/child relationship and things are somewhat different nowadays. Regardless, to this day I still move quickly when my mother asks me to do something for her. It's just how I am wired. I am not sure that same fear exists in today's youth. Either way, my children came from my gene pool, so what happened? Here's what I believe: Societal evolution and new variables like advances in technology (good or bad) have created generational differences in how we interact with the world around us.

Do you think there is a difference in the way generations perceive and manage their time (work and play)? In a recent discussion (September, 2015) with graduate students representing a variety of generations, along with an open discussion using social media

(LinkedIn and Facebook), I posed this question. Here are some of the responses:

- *Most definitely!! Today's generation spends all their time on computer games and cell phones...they don't get outside and enjoy real life and adventures. They have no imagination and even less motivation. Their communication skills are almost non-existent. They don't have to think for themselves because all they have to do is hit Google or ask Siri or Pandora or whomever. Technology has helped us to raise a generation of individuals who are very literate when it comes to electronic devices, but absolutely illiterate when it comes to dealing with another human individual or group. Children are not raised to respect their parents, teachers, or any of their elders. Time out seriously needs to go away. I am a child of the '50s.*

- *My generation (37 yrs. old) is under a tremendous amount of pressure...with no clear role to follow. We are 'forced' to be everything—providers, caregivers, and drivers, etc. We are also trying to raise today's generation. I do believe many of us have to rely on electronics, due to the pressures of having two working parents, crazy schedules, and so on...but, there are still many of us who are instilling traditional values in our children or trying to. I would say we are collectively...confused...and TIRED!*

- *The old ideas of going to work and then going home are no longer valid. Work happens at home, in the coffee shop, and on our commute. And social life happens at work. Tell a Gen-Xer that you'll not tolerate Facebook/Instagram/Pinterest at work and they'll find another job. They expect to be in constant communication with their social network and they won't tolerate anything less. A job or even jobs are just one more item that Gen-X juggles around. They think in terms of "gigs," wherein they attach themselves to this group for this time and then move on to another group. It's best to understand they are always at work and always also not at work. As an employer you can measure and insist on the output, but you are less in control of how/where the work is accomplished. In my father's day the boss could tell if he was working. If he was working the machine in front of him was cranking out product. Now the young woman in the coffee shop in sandals listening to her headphones MIGHT be your most productive employee, and the bolt-straight-up shirt and tie guy sitting diligently at his desk for 40 hours might be the least effective. (Boomer)*

- *I am nearing 50 and work with mid-30-year-olds. There is definitely a difference. These 30-somethings are children of the Boomers. The Boomers changed the world and my generation is caught in the middle. You work hard; you respect and learn from the generation before. The mid-30 generation wants the best (like their parents). They are the technology generation and want automation. They will get ahead without the help of generations previous to them if they have to. They want flexibility. They don't want to sit in an office. They want to focus on their passion. The generation who is retiring is challenged because "they did their time" and they just want to ride it out. Sometimes it is hard to change and adapt when you have been doing it that way for so long and you only have bit more to go. That generation is also struggling because their plans to retire early have shifted for them because they must work longer to qualify for benefits like Social Security.*

- *I do. I believe that individuals of my generation and the generations that follow value their "play" time more, and actively seek to achieve a good work/life balance. I notice this regularly in my graduate class: Although we are all actively seeking jobs and very busy with our studies, we prioritize giving ourselves periods of free time throughout the week, especially on the weekends. Whether we have families or not, it is a way for us to keep our sanity amidst our crazy schedules. In fact, I think my generation actively seeks to carve out time during the week that is free of work, whereas in past generations people have focused more on getting as much work in as possible.*

- *Yes. Older generations held a stronger belief in work/life balance. I believe that now there is an image of the ideal worker norm that demands employed individuals to devote themselves fully to work, placing work at the top of the priority list. It was possible and accepted in the past to leave work at five and hang up your coat. Now, we are working nearly around the clock to manage the expectations of our employers and get ahead in the workplace. (Graduate student)*

In a study on generations and perceived time by Bergmann, Lester, and De Meuse, their findings revealed a significant relationship between age and employment status. Younger workers (25-44 years of age) were more likely to be employed part-time in an attempt to improve their quality of life (defined by the workers as more downtime). Older workers (45 years of age and above) worked more full-time to improve their quality of life (defined by the workers as financial stability).[8]

Our perception of time, and how we choose to prioritize its use, seems to be directly related to what we value. Multiple researchers proclaim that what we value is age-related.

Generational Traits and Expectations in the Workplace

Generation	Traits	Expectations
Traditionalists	Dedicated Hardworking Conformist Respect for authority Duty before pleasure	Security from the organization Promotion based on longevity Wait for instructions
Baby Boomers	Optimistic Team-oriented Involved in planning Seek personal growth	Live to work Pursuit of goals Accepts but does not embrace change
Generation X	Values diversity Thinks globally Technically literate Self-reliant	Works to live Promotion based on ability Expects to provide input
Millennials	Optimistic Confident Street smart Social	Multitaskers Hardworking Prefers structure Respects position

Source: Adapted from Patota, Schwartz, and Schwartz (2007)[9]

Despite these differences in perceived values, there are a number of places where Baby Boomers and Millennials are actually in agreement. Among the results of a survey released by Workfront and conducted online by Harris Poll are the following findings:

- **It's your party...but I couldn't show up if I wanted to.** Millennials (54 percent) and Baby Boomers (53 percent) both said they have missed important life events because of work. They also both agreed that one of the more negative consequences of having a bad work/life balance was their inability to fully focus when they were actually with family because they were still thinking about work (Millennials 43 percent vs. Baby Boomers 39 percent).

- **I'll have a side of "off the clock" for dinner.** Both groups agree (Millennials 56 percent vs. Baby Boomers 58 percent) that technology has ruined the modern dinnertime. Baby Boomers (85 percent) and Millennials (88 percent) also agree that it's important for employers to respect their time off the clock.

- **Will yoga make my work schedule more flexible?** When asked to name what had the most negative effect on an employee's work/life balance, Millennials (35 percent) and Baby Boomers (39 percent) agreed that inflexibility in work schedules played a big part. Not surprisingly, both groups said flexible work schedules would make their work/life balance better (Millennials 72 percent vs. Baby Boomers 71 percent).[10]

No matter which generation we belong to, time is an important issue for most of us. But our perspective on time could very well be influenced by our generational affiliation. It could also be influenced by a broader sense of how we see the world. For example, are you future-oriented or do you prefer to live "in the moment"? A future-oriented person may be more concerned about working for future goals and rewards, often at the expense of present enjoyment, whereas someone who lives in the moment may choose to spend their time on those activities that offer immediate gratification.

Of course, there are also those rare people with a balanced time perspective who seem to adjust to the situation they find themselves in. When they spend time with their families and friends, they are fully with them, connecting and enjoying each other. When they take a day off work, they can rest rather than feel restless. However, when working and studying, they approach a situation from the perspective of the future and work more productively. Although some of us may not be able to achieve this level of balance in our lives, we can all certainly tweak our imbalances in order to elevate us to a better place.

In regard to the perception of time, your generation matters somewhat, but it is not the whole story. A complex web of variables influences how we choose to manage our time (or whether we let time control us). There are no doubt lessons that each generation can teach us, and in some cases, we can even learn what not to do by a given generation's shortcomings. Don't worry too much that the year you were born has trapped you into the wrong mindset. Just be aware of why you view time management the way you do. This prepares you to make better decisions moving forward. Boom!

"Make up your mind to this. If you are different, you are isolated, not only from people of your own age but from those of your parents' generation and from your children's generation too. They'll never understand you and they'll be shocked no matter what you do. But your grandparents would probably be proud of you and say: 'There's a chip off the old block,' and your grandchildren will sigh enviously and say: 'What an old rip Grandma must have been!' and they'll try to be like you."

—Margaret Mitchell

Motherhood Ate My Minutes!

"He who every morning plans the transaction of the day and follows out that plan, carries a thread that will guide him through the maze of the most busy life. But where no plan is laid, where the disposal of time is surrendered merely to the chance of incidence, chaos will soon reign."

—Victor Hugo

Time management is a big concern for mothers these days. Between kids' activities, household responsibilities, and, for many, the demands of a stressful workplace, many mothers have given up on the fight to find time for themselves and are just trying to get everything done. Even though the roles for spouses are becoming more blurred, women are still in the majority when it comes to managing the home and kids.

According to the Pew Research Center, mothers and fathers spend roughly the same total amount of time working, although men's time is more apt to be spent in work outside the home, while women still do more housework and child care. And, a convergence in gender roles among married couples seems to have slowed over the past 20 years.

While mothers and fathers spend about the same amount of time on paid work, household work, and childcare combined, these types of work may not be created equal. Even the types of childcare that mothers and fathers give are different. Fathers spend a greater percentage of their childcare time playing with children, while mothers spend greater percentages of this time giving physical care such as bathing or feeding children. Similarly, men in the American Time Use Survey found household cleaning to be more stressful than women did. So, although the total number of hours that parents spend on making the family run may be roughly equivalent, the amount of energy it takes to do so may not be the same.[11]

In her book, *Working Mom's 411: How to Manage Kids, Career & Home,* author Michelle LaRowe notes that many moms with full-time jobs are left with about 40 hours a week to get all of these things accomplished:

- Clean the house

- Do laundry

- Shop for groceries

- Take care of errands, which may include paying bills and handling financial matters

- Help kids with homework

- Be present at kids' activities

- Spend time with partner

- Spend time with friends and family members

- Pursue personal interests of any kind

- And "maybe—just maybe—sneak in an hour to go to the gym or to soak in a bubble bath"[12]

No wonder so many women I know are so tired!

Anna's story below offers insight into the normal daily routine for many working moms. It gives a whole new meaning to "do-it-all woman." I asked Anna to describe her typical day:

My name is Anna. I'm 37 years old, a mom of four children. I have two boys, Anthony Jr., 19, and Cristian, 17, and two girls, Brianna, 15, and Jessica, 8. I have been married 19-and-a-half years to the love of my life. It hasn't always been roses, but we have made it and we couldn't love each other more than we do now.

My alarm goes off at 4:50 a.m. I wake my 15-year-old up for school and set my alarm for 5:25 a.m. That's when I wake up my 17-year-old. Then I go back to bed to get a few more minutes of sleep before my hectic day "begins."

Once 6:00 a.m. rolls around I get up and quickly get ready for work. I'm rushing because I know I'm on a schedule. As soon as I'm dressed, I wake up my 8-year-old. Next it's time to go downstairs to get breakfast started and make lunch for the kids and myself. My oldest son gets home from work with my car (he works nights) and then I dash out the door.

Once I'm in the car, I call my husband, who's already on his way to work. This is one of the few times we get to really talk during the day so we use this time to catch up.

Finally, I get to work. I am a receptionist for a family practice—a very unorganized family practice. When I arrive there are already patients waiting to be checked in and the phones are ringing off the hook. I set my stuff down and don't even get a chance to breathe. Despite the (many) stresses of a typical workplace environment, I continue to do my job to the best of my ability. The patients love me and I love them, but deep down inside I know it's time to find a new job.

By the time lunchtime rolls around, I'm exhausted. Usually my husband calls me while I'm eating lunch in my car and I talk to him until it's time to go back upstairs. The afternoons at work can be just as hectic. I'm looking at the clock and waiting for 4:30 to roll around. On my way home, my mind is still racing from my hectic work day. I just want to get home!

Once home, it's time to start dinner. When that's underway, I make myself a protein shake. After I drink it, I go upstairs to change my clothes and get my playlist together for class, because I teach Zumba Monday through Thursday. Sometimes, I am not in the mood for Zumba, so I try to work myself up on the way there. But once class starts, I always get lost in the music, just the way I like it.

I get home and the kitchen is still a mess from dinner. Time to make sure Jess is showered and ready for bed. Then it's shower time for me, and afterward I throw a load of laundry into the wash (which never gets put away, but is thrown into the laundry basket). Once that's all done, I finally lay down for bed and start thinking about tomorrow.

As Anna's story shows us, time management can be one of the most difficult skills to master. Even the most organized person will become stressed out when short on time. From doing their best each day at work, to spending quality time with their children after the workday is over, working mothers must have a plan to accomplish all the tasks on their ever-increasing to-do lists. While other chapters later in this book will offer detailed tips, here are a few key tips for mothers trying to maximize their minutes:

- **Minimize distractions and the tendency to multitask.** Instead, focus on each daily task one at a time. For example, if you are working on a project for work, don't start thinking about the dinner menu. You will find the task at hand will take longer.

- **Set reasonable daily goals—we *are not* superheroes.** Record events in a calendar, if needed, to keep track of activities. This will allow you to prioritize, delegate, or just ditch the activity altogether. A planning notebook can be your best friend. Keep a notebook that has a calendar and a space for notes, appointments, to-do lists, etc. Commit yourself to writing in it and referring to it daily. A good place to begin is by writing birthdays, anniversaries, and other special dates. From there you can include school plays, piano recitals, vacations, dentist and doctor appointments, and other key commitments.

- **Learn to say "no."** It's okay to turn down invitations, cancel plans, or to disconnect from the outside world every now and then. You don't have to attend every PTA meeting or head up every committee in town. Even though it can be hard at first, learning to say no is a valuable skill that will benefit you for the rest of your life.

• **Don't seek perfectionism.** Sometimes we mothers believe we have to be all things to all people. We have feelings of guilt when we don't live up to this self-imposed standard or when we cannot get everything done in a 24-hour day. Check your expectations. Do you expect your house to look like a picture from a magazine even though you have three young children? If so, you'll have to realize your expectations just aren't in line with reality. A home where children live, learn, and play is bound to have that "lived in" look. That's okay. Don't look back on these years with your children at home and regret that you spent most of it worrying about having things perfect. Give yourself permission to be less than perfect. The vacuuming can wait another day or can be done by someone else.

We have established just how time-consuming and stressful motherhood can be. Don't resign yourself to a frantic and stressed out existence just yet though—motherhood is supposed to be a joyous experience! Understand that learning to manage your time efficiently is the key to getting everything done on time and with grace. You can conquer motherhood and even become a "supermom" of sorts (whatever that means!).

So, When Do We Play?

"We don't stop playing because we grow old; we grow old because we stop playing."
—George Bernard Shaw

In the hustle of everyday life, many of us focus so heavily on work and family commitments that we never seem to have time for pure fun. When is the last time you laughed or did something that made you forget, even for a moment, the stressors in your life? This could be anything, such as a great movie with your spouse or significant other, an exercise class, or the amusement park with your kids. If you're like many people, you probably can't even remember the last time you did something just for the fun of it.

So when are we supposed to carve out some leisure time? We're more likely to zone out in front of the TV or computer rather than engage in fun, rejuvenating play like we did when we were children. Somewhere between childhood and adulthood, we stopped playing. But just because we're now adults, that doesn't mean we have to take ourselves so seriously and make life all about work. We still need time to play so that we can mentally and physically recharge. Play time can add joy to your life, relieve stress, supercharge learning, and connect you to others and the world around you. What a great use of your hot minutes. Best of all, play may even add days to your life!

Finding the time to play will mean moving it up on your list of priorities. We often relegate play to the optional category. Some have even forgotten how good it feels to let go and have fun. However, once you discover the stress-relieving power of play time, you will find a way to squeeze it in!

Kim's story:

Twelve years ago at our wedding, we received a check for a gift from family friends made out to "Kim and Tim oh my God that rhymes!" It really said that! I always said I searched long and hard to find a Tim to match my name, and thank God he turned out great! He's even better than great: He's my partner in all things life. Now with a 7- and 4.5-year-old, our lives never contain a dull moment.

I am a planner. Tim is not. But, without fail, every week we sit and plan our dinners, our kids' activities, our workouts, and our evening fun. The idea of getting it all done is really overwhelming. So I write daily lists that help me focus on the now.

However, focusing on now doesn't mean you can't also plan for the future. We're the couple who has those yearly life-goal discussions. It usually takes place on one of our day trip adventures where we are in the car for hours. We reevaluate our needs and wants, and when I tell you they change, I mean they really change!

On one of our weekend adventures exploring our state, North Carolina, we designed a game plan for what we now refer to as "The Year of Kim." I had some goals I wanted to address. I was itching to start designing again. Plus, I had gained weight that I hoped to lose. Finally, I wanted to meet new friends as I didn't know many people in our new state. So the kids' coloring book we had in the car became a fascinating outline of what needed to be done.

I love my gym. It's a small, family-owned joint with a plethora of classes. The energetic side of me jumped at the chance to try all different types of classes. The schedule was a dream as I could choose classes when both kids were in school or after they were in bed. My planner was riddled with gym classes and my body changed rapidly. I allotted one hour of time for myself a day when my body would sweat out the stress and pound away any anxiety I had from work's demands. I went all in knowing each jumping jack or bicep curl was my ticket to achieving laser focus with my family and my work. And all the hard work lifted me into a better version of myself.

Tim loved the changes in my confidence and energy level, and proudly held my new muscles up to the kids for a lesson in perseverance. Then he said, "I want muscles like my wife." Thus, operation "Get Tim to the Gym" was born.

Tim and I realize where our support needs to shift. An ebb and flow, a give and take, or a push and pull. We never stop our own dreams, but our family is a unit, and in order for our family to be first, our support for each other's dreams needs to be respected. I love supporting my husband, and he loves supporting me. It's our desire to see each other succeed.

This past September Tim and I jumped over the fire at the finish line of our very first Spartan Race. It's an obstacle course race where you battle your own strength, desire, and determination.

We kissed the medals we won and then each other, proud of conquering that goal together.

Goal-oriented people are driven. Driven people are passionate. Tim and I are immersed in the worlds of our passions. Whether that is fitness or art or our boys. Our friends are driven like we are, and the husbands support the wives and the wives the husbands. Our circle is a palette of like-minded couples and individuals who awe us with every new bend in life's road. We learn from each other, thrive off of each other, and motivate one another.

When we go in, we go all in. There is no half way. If it's important to Tim, it's important to me and reverse. It's not life's balance we worry about; it's our family balance that matters. Seeing our children's faces at the end of the race was empowering. Tackling that goal head-on was exhilarating. We made time for ourselves and that taught our children a lesson. That anything is possible.

—Submitted by Kim Saguinsin

There are two clear takeaways from Kim's story: First, you *CAN* find the time for anything, as long as it's something you value and if you have the support of significant people in your life. The second takeaway is that with each step of Kim and Tim's journey, they gained momentum and energy. Their success is inspiring.

Play Time at Work

As I enter the conference center, I hear the music before I round the corner. Festive Caribbean drums, a photo station set up like the front of a ship, and greeters dressed in cruise wear immediately change my mood and expectations for the day. Non-alcoholic drinks with tiny umbrellas and tables bedecked with palm trees fill the room. Who would have guessed the "Our Journey to Excellence" conference would capture the essence of a tropical sea cruise? Wow!

The conference organizers know the secret. If you want to hold people's attention for a whole day of intense learning, play must be a part of the equation. When you play, you engage the creative side of your brain. This can often help you see challenges in a new light and generate fresh, creative solutions.

Infusing appropriate play into the workplace can promote a positive culture, which leads to improved productivity and stronger relationships. Some fun ways to marry work and play:

- Basketball hoop in the parking lot
- Themed business meetings (sometimes employees are even encouraged to dress for the theme)
- Treadmill stations or on-site fitness centers
- Treasure hunts in the office (these could be related to key business initiatives)
- Birthday and holiday celebrations

These are just a few simple ideas. Can you think of others?

In this chapter we have explored many variables impacting our perceptions of how we spend our time and our capacity to do more. The common themes around the balance between work and play, motherhood, technology, and generational differences are *choice* and *sacrifice*. We all own the choices and sacrifices we make that could lead us to a more balanced lifestyle. By taking control of those choices and investing in what we value, our precious minutes are well spent. In the next chapter, we will explore "time robbers" that could be hindering you from making the right choices for your life.

"You couldn't change history. But you could get it right to start with. Do something differently the FIRST time around. This whole business with seeking Slytherin's secrets... seemed an awful lot like the sort of thing where, years later, you would look back and say, 'And THAT was where it all started to go wrong.' And he would wish desperately for the ability to fall back through time and make a different choice. Wish granted. Now what?"

—Eliezer Yudkowsky, *Harry Potter and the Methods of Rationality*

CHAPTER TWO:

Time Robbers: Stealing Our Lives One "Hot Minute" at a Time

"Yesterday's the past, tomorrow's the future, but today is a gift. That's why it's called the present."

—Bil Keane

What Is the Most Valuable Thing on Earth?

I believe most of us would agree that the answer to this question is *time*. Everything in life is acquired *in* time and conducted *by* time. You could have food, clothing, fabulous homes, and endless wisdom, but without time to experience and enjoy it all, you might as well have nothing. Yet too often we seem to squander the very thing we should value the most. We allow various "time robbers" to take away pieces of our lives.

What are time robbers? They are the people or the things that distract us from achieving what we set out to do. In the long run, we lose pieces of ourselves along the way.

I wonder if we would be more mindful of the time we spend on wasteful activities if we thought about time the same way we think about our money—as a form of currency. If "time" could somehow replace cold hard cash in our checking accounts, would our daily choices be any different than they are now? Think of it this way: If you and your family continually come up short on funds at the end of each month, you must eventually sit down and analyze your spending, identify where your money is going, create appropriate solutions, and then adjust your spending habits accordingly.

When my grandson wants an expensive pair of sneakers and my checkbook indicates "no way!"—even though I may disappoint him—I have no trouble making this decision so I can buy groceries instead. We can and should manage our time the same way. Yet often, when it comes to time, we buy not only the (metaphorical) "sneakers" but also the "workout clothes" to match. In other words, we overextend ourselves even though we know it is not in our best interest. And in turn, the quality of our lives come up short—just like our overextended checkbooks.

Why do we wastefully fritter away time then? I truthfully don't believe people are lazy and I don't believe they don't care. What I do believe is that most people think that they will be able to "catch up" on all their lost minutes somewhere down the road. It's so easy to get caught up in various time-wasting activities or to spend all of our time worrying about the wrong things. This lost time adds up. We take for granted those precious minutes that we can never recover, and this ultimately takes a toll on our present and our future.

In order to get your life back one minute at a time, you need to identify your own personal time robbers. This chapter will focus on a few of the most common ones people experience and offer some useful strategies to consider in reclaiming *your* minutes. I think of these time robbers as the "big four." They are:

- Poor listening
- Becoming sheep
- Moving papers
- Misaligned or changing priorities

Other time robbers will be covered in more detail in upcoming chapters. These include:

- Electronics
- Constant crises at home and work
- Meetings without purpose
- Disorganization
- Poor communication
- Unclear responsibility and authority
- Procrastination/indecision
- Ineffective delegation
- Inability to say no
- Multitasking

A few of these time robbers truly do exist outside of our control. Occasionally an emergency does strike out of the blue. Sometimes we are required to attend meetings that we know are pointless. But I believe in most cases there *are* things we can do to prevent these time robbers from showing up in our lives—and to disarm them when they do rear their heads.

What Did You Say? The Art of Active Listening

It's 7:00 p.m. and I am exhausted from a workday that never seemed to end. Now it's time to finally sit down, eat a good meal, and relax. (At least that was the plan in my head.) But I can't turn off my mind! Thoughts from the last meeting of the day and what I need to do in the morning keep haunting me. *World News Tonight* on television distracts me for a minute; however, I am sure I would fail the test on what is actually reported. And, there sitting beside me is my dear husband, trying to communicate something important to me about his day. (Hopefully he doesn't quiz me later on our chat, because I would surely fail that test as well!)

This is an all-too-common scenario. When I am overwhelmed, it's as if my ability to *actively listen* completely goes away. Even during times when I should be relaxing and spending quality moments with my loved ones, the incessant urge to multitask robs me of those precious minutes. My husband cringes in utter frustration when I ask for the third time, *"What did you say?"*

Poor communication is a major time robber. We spend so much time communicating with others, but when we don't *actively listen*, we miss out on valuable information and our various relationships suffer as a result. Poor communication leads to:

- Rework—because of lack of clarity in expectations or roles

- Rebuilding relationships strained by poor communication

- Repeating an entire conversation because we did not hear it the first time or we misinterpreted the bits and pieces we did hear

Here are some characteristics of active versus inactive listening:

ACTIVE LISTENING	INACTIVE LISTENING
Listens closely for information that can be important and useful.	Becomes distanced from the listening experience, loses focus, daydreams, chats, or sleeps.
Continually refocuses attention on the speaker, knowing that attention may sometimes wander.	Is present in body but not mind.
Filters out distractions and concentrates on what's being said.	Uses distractions as an excuse to stop listening.
Body language denotes engagement (positioning that faces the speaker, eye contact, nodding of head to acknowledge attention).	Body language denotes distraction.
Listens very carefully to understand the speaker's point of view before challenging what is said. Limits interruptions.	Gets upset at words that trigger certain emotions and stops listening. Constantly interrupts.
Can accurately repeat back what has been said (monitoring tone to reflect the intensity and content of what was heard). Asks clarifying questions.	Guesses content shared by picking up on a few key words that were heard (usually inaccurate in content and intent).

Research suggests that we remember between 25 and 50 percent of what we hear. That means that when you talk to your boss, colleagues, customers, or spouse for 10 minutes, they pay attention to less than half of the conversation.

Now conversely, this research reveals that you most likely aren't getting the whole message either. Think about your conversations and ask yourself whether you consistently retain the information you receive. Hopefully you are retaining the important stuff. But chances are you are missing 25 to 50 percent of your information like the rest of us.

Clearly, active listening is a skill that we can all benefit from. By becoming a better listener, you increase your productivity, as well as your ability to influence, persuade, and negotiate. What's more, you'll avoid conflict and misunderstandings on a personal and professional level.

Understand that old habits are hard to break. It takes a lot of concentration and determination to be an active listener, and you may find your focus drifting in and out during your communications with others. Most people have to work really hard to minimize this time robber's influence over them.

A few tips that may help:

- Value the minutes spent in conversation with others. Remind yourself that having this person in your life is a gift. Remind yourself that you love, like, or need this person.

- Be deliberate when you are listening and remind yourself frequently that your goal is to truly hear what the other person is saying to you. Set aside all other thoughts and behaviors and concentrate on the message at hand.

- If you feel your mind wandering away from the conversation, gently guide yourself back to the present.

- Ask questions, reflect, and paraphrase to ensure you understand the message. Anything less is a waste of time.

"The most basic of all human needs is the need to understand and be understood. The best way to understand people is to listen to them."

— Ralph Nichols

Baaaaa Behavior: Is Your Inner Sheep Running Your Life?

"To be yourself in a world that is constantly trying to make you something else is the greatest accomplishment."

— Ralph Waldo Emerson

Have you ever heard or maybe even uttered one of the following sentences yourself?

"We've always done it this way." or *"Everyone else is going, so I must attend."*

In an attempt to stay mainstream or not rock the boat, we often allow ourselves to become sheep. Even if we have a diverging point of view or would rather spend our time differently, we remain quiet on the surface. In doing so, we relinquish control of our time in order to maintain the status quo. I call this tendency to "follow the herd" *sheep behavior*, and it is yet another time robber that you should be aware of.

We all have been in situations where we got swept up by the behavior of the crowd. Here are some examples:

Most of your coworkers have signed up for the annual 5k run set for this Saturday. However, you've scheduled a long overdue spa date with yourself (after a grueling work week) for the same time as the event. You believe it's a great cause and a fun opportunity to hang out with your coworkers, but you've been looking forward to your spa day. The pressure is enormous for you to attend the 5k, even though it is optional and you really don't like running. Mental and emotional conflict ensues. You go to the 5k and give up the time you had allotted for self-care. If only you had more time to do both. *"Baaaaa."*

You are a busy physician in a group medical practice. Administration is constantly monitoring productivity as an indicator of your performance. As a five-year veteran at the clinic, you have established a rhythm of seeing patients that matches the other physicians. Now, all of you are asked to adjust in order to keep up with the productivity requirements. No one wants to change from the way they have always worked. A new physician leader has been hired who brings new tools and tactics to advance efficiency and patient flow. Even though you are curious about new ways to improve, you won't go against your colleagues. *"We have always done it this way…no need to change. Baaaaa."*

In each example, we sacrificed time, our needs, or our beliefs in order to follow the group norm. At times, following the norm is acceptable and encouraged. This is especially true when executing best practices in the workplace intended to save time and increase quality. In order to achieve consistency across the workforce, it's okay to be a sheep. However, when following the norm goes against efficiency or desirable outcomes and is in conflict with your values, you must become your own "shepherd" and do what's best for you.

Remember, we are in charge of our lives and it is entirely up to us whether we create our own path or stay safe by doing what others do. In addition to controlling how you spend your time, here are some additional reasons why you should consider being very selective about when you choose to be a sheep:

- People who have achieved massive success and fortune aren't like other people. They have become who they are today because they dared to be different. Otherwise, everyone would be a millionaire.

- Following the crowd will make you settle for what you think is good enough.

- Following the crowd can limit, if not stop, your potential for growth. If you live your life according to what you see as normal from other people, the possibility of fulfilling your personal dreams and goals will be very small.

"The person who follows the crowd will usually go no further than the crowd. The person who walks alone is likely to find himself in places no one has ever seen before."

— Albert Einstein

Moving Papers: The Never-Ending Task

One time, two times, six times, more
How many times before walking out the door
Paper, paper everywhere
Document checking—what a scare
Why can't just one touch suffice?
Then file away—that's my advice
But paranoia takes control
And one more touch now takes a toll
Wasted time in paper hell
I need action to ring the bell!

—Jackie Gaines

Most of us waste a lot of time shuffling paper from one pile to another on our desks. Do you really need a pending tray? Chances are it is full of paper that you don't know what to do with! Even if you decide to file away a particular piece of paper, you may find that you never look at it again. So is it really necessary to keep it or should you go ahead and toss it? Moving the same paper over and over is a time robber for most people.

As an aspiring leader in nursing (much earlier in my career), I wanted to advance to the role of "head nurse." Today they would call this role a nurse manager or director. At Johns Hopkins Hospital, where I worked, the only way you got advanced into a leadership role in nursing was to pass the Nurse Leader Assessment Center.

There were multiple pre-set stations placing you in situations common for nursing leaders. You were judged on your proficiency, agility, and efficiency in completing the assigned task. Time management was seen as a value for any leader. One of the stations included a desk full of papers, a calendar, empty file folders, and empty bins, including a trash bin. We were given 15 minutes to decide how to best organize the paper and associated tasks by their relevance. The papers included junk mail, policies, memos from employees, and more.

I remember thinking, *How on earth will I ever organize all of this in 15 minutes?* Surely, they will ask me to leave the Assessment Center for failing to figure this out. I took a deep breath and remembered the *golden rule* I heard somewhere: "Touch paper only once, then do something!"

I did pass the Assessment Center (whew!) but walked away knowing this ability to manage paper efficiently was a career skill I would need to work on. It probably wouldn't be bad for my personal life either. I also wondered how many people waste valuable minutes manipulating inanimate objects, like paper, instead of spending it interacting with each other—a critical success factor for any relationship.

A simple exercise to see if you are falling into the trap of moving papers around your desk is to place a dot in the corner of the page every time you pick up a piece of paper, and see how many dots you end up with before you take action and deal with it. This exercise includes mail piled up in your virtual world—notice how long it takes you to delete the spam that gathers in your inbox.

Let's assume that you've started clearing out some of the papers that keep piling up, but still you just can't help yourself. There is still that one piece of paper (or five!) that you simply can't get rid of. You just keep looking at that piece of paper. Sometimes you clear off all the paper from your desk and that one piece is still in the to-do pile. You can feel your frustration mounting higher right along with your stack of paper! Something's gotta give!

So, how do you practice the art of touching a piece of paper only once?

When you receive a piece of paper, either in the post or via e-mail, you should do one of the following things immediately:

- Get rid of the to-do pile. Otherwise it only gets bigger.

- Act on it. Decide whether you will act on an issue or not. Remember, it's okay to say no.

- File it. Some paper we need to maintain for proof of documentation, but you don't need to file everything. Do you have five-year-old receipts in a drawer somewhere? Toss 'em!

- Delegate it to someone else. Many papers require someone else's action before you can conclude yours. Whether you need someone else to complete an action or you need something as simple as a signature, delegate that piece of paper immediately.

- Throw it away. Dispose of non-essential papers. (You should keep forms regarding taxes, warranties, or papers with original signatures.) Delete junk e-mails and throw away junk mail as soon as it is received. If you get stuck, ask yourself, *What is the worst thing that would happen if I did not have this paper?*

Misaligned Priorities: Do You Know What You Really, Really Want?

"How did it get so late so soon? It's night before it's afternoon. December is here before it's June. My goodness how the time has flown. How did it get so late so soon?"

—Dr. Seuss

Nothing good ever comes from a call from your children at 3:00 a.m. As soon as the phone's ring jerks you awake, your heart races and your groggy mind starts imagining all kinds of horrific reasons for such a call. Are they hurt? Did someone die? Immediately you answer the phone and know that soon you will have to reprioritize everything else that may be on your to-do list that day to deal with whatever the crisis may be. At that moment your priorities are your kids, and everything else becomes less important.

Isn't it funny how quickly we can prioritize everything in a real or perceived crisis, yet struggle doing the same thing with our precious minutes on any given day? We make excuses as to why less important things rob us of our time. We even put off things like doctor's appointments, which are intended to give us *more* minutes on this planet. We need a priority "tune-up," starting with setting realistic goals for ourselves on both personal and professional levels.

Begin by looking at your life in small chunks. This kind of retrospective look back can be overwhelming if we try and look at the whole year—so break it into manageable pieces. Take into consideration how you spent your time over the past three months. Now ask yourself the following:

- What would you keep doing?

- What would you want to eliminate or stop doing?

- What's missing that you might want to add?

Now using that list, create goals for the upcoming three months. Be as specific as you can, using action-oriented words. Try to separate professional goals from personal ones. Select three or four priorities that rise to the top of your list and make a commitment to keep them front and center over the next three months. Treat them with the same urgency as you would a crisis—like a 3:00 a.m. call from a loved one. Don't try to save the world. It's always important to be realistic about what you can accomplish in three months. And remember that success begets more success, so start small and you can gradually work up to larger goals.

Here are some examples:

- If you want to run a marathon, find one right now and put a deadline on signing up and coordinating with friends in your calendar.

- If you want to learn a new skill, figure out what you need to do to accomplish that goal. Who are the people you need to call upon for help? Schedule the necessary calls and training.

- If you have no "me" time built into your day, pencil in small amounts of time just for you, the same way you would schedule an appointment. Block it out and try not to relinquish it for other things. Even 15 minutes set aside offers you time to breathe, relax, or do a quick self-assessment.

If your goals are clear and specific, you should be able to check them off your list and move on to the next three months with new hills to climb. You will feel a wonderful sense of accomplishment as you conquer your goals one chunk at a time and release more and more of the time-robbing misaligned priorities that once held you captive.

The only way to gain control over the time robbers in your life is to *stop giving them power!* Get back in the driver's seat and take charge of the time robbers that you can actually control. Don't rationalize poor choices you've made in the past and continue to live with them; they will silently defeat you. Instead, make better choices each day as you move forward to improve the quality of minutes you have.

CHAPTER THREE:

Maximizing Your Minutes: Tips for Effective Time Management

> *"Time is the most valuable coin in your life. You and you alone will determine how that coin will be spent. Be careful that you do not let other people spend it for you."*
> — Carl Sandburg

Reflect, Prioritize, Act

Self-awareness is always step one in any personal improvement journey. So, here's a quick self-test to see how you currently spend your time in a typical day. Remember, the total hours cannot exceed 24! Once you have listed your activity hours, attempt to rank them from highest to lowest priority, with number one being the highest priority in your life on most days.

Don't assume that you already know where all of your time goes. Our perceptions of how we spend time usually appear badly distorted when we actually compare them using detailed analysis. Be sure to be honest when building your time log! Don't kid yourself when you record your activities, or your data will be of little use.

Activity/Task	Number of Hours	Priority Rank
Sleeping		
Eating		
Self-care		
Exercise		
Personal time (just you)		
Focused shared time with significant others (family, friends)		
TV or other forms of entertainment		
Connected to electronic devices (phones, Internet)		
Work		
Studying		
Personal work (cleaning, repairs, cooking…)		
	MUST TOTAL 24 HOURS	

Was this activity easy or difficult? Many people find this exercise both frustrating and eye-opening. We live our lives amidst competing number-one priorities daily, hourly, and sometimes even minute to minute. However, if everything we do feels like a number-one priority, is it even possible that *anything* we do is a true priority? We usually don't hit the pause button long enough to reflect on our daily choices and what *should be* the top priority because it is the most important thing in our lives. We usually just stay stuck in *doing*, even when our actions do not move us closer to our goals.

After the true "time robbers" are identified from your analysis, pick one or two that are the most wasteful. Then look for a few simple remedies to reduce these "time robbers." Planning your day, ranking priorities, controlling interruptions, setting aside stated office hours, or shortening your meetings may be among your possible remedies.

Whatever you do, be sure not to rely on others to determine your time priorities. You are the only person who is qualified to judge the importance of all the things you must achieve in a given day.

Ask yourself: *Would you rather complete less important tasks and be busy and stressed all the time, or would you rather focus on what's important, caring less for the nonessentials, and have a more relaxing life?*

Ask yourself: *Is this task important or urgent?*

Importance is defined as "the state or fact of being of great significance or value."[1] Urgency is defined as "a force or impulse that impels or constrains."[2] I believe that we often confuse importance with urgency. This causes us to respond as if everything is "on fire" and requires our immediate response or attention.

Not all things we perceive as urgent are important. Level of urgency is useful for choosing what we spend our energy on each day. However, ultimately the level of importance that any task or action has in our lives should be the key driver in the choices we make. When importance drives our decisions, we can usually find a way to deal with the urgency factor.

Here are some examples to consider:

An e-mail from work hits your inbox just as you sit down for a nice evening meal with your family. This is usually sacred time for you to relax, listen to their stories, and center yourself after the craziness of your day.

You hear the computer's "bing" alerting you of the e-mail's arrival just as the mashed potatoes are passed your way. Every part of you knows it's from work with a new deadline or operational update you need to view and respond to. You immediately wonder how you will fit this interruption into an already planned evening with family.

By the time the chicken reaches your plate, you are completely distracted and now feel compelled to read the e-mail. The urgency builds as dinner progresses and the importance of family fades with each course of the meal.

Finally, you excuse yourself and check the e-mail. You confirm that there is indeed a new deadline and now you must figure out your response.

Now, here are your possible choices:

- Ditch dinner and do it now! (Urgency wins.)
- Acknowledge the task, tuck it away mentally, and prioritize work in the morning. (Importance of focused family time is considered.)

- Best response: Put the computer/phone in another room so you never hear the sound in the first place. You choose to have a focus on family from the beginning of dinner. Work can resume in the morning. (Importance wins!)

But what if you fear that ignoring the e-mail could affect your job security? You could handle this by taking a more proactive approach and defining expectations with your boss around responding to e-mails and calls after normal work hours. You may be surprised to find that your assumptions about urgency may not be aligned with hers.

Urgent issues should be rare and could ideally be identified as such in the subject line of the e-mail—allowing you to know exactly when it is imperative for you to respond. However, if the frequency of urgent issues increases to weekly or more, then the problem is not just when to respond but the need to define the source of challenges placing you and the organization in a state of constant reactivity. That's a very different but important conversation about organizational priorities and how to be more proactive in order to limit the constant state of crisis.

Now, here is another example:

Saturday mornings are sheer chaos and confusion at your house. Between your two children, there are a variety of extracurricular activities that (of course) fall at conflicting times, and you have only one vehicle.

If you choose to miss one child's activity, he will be disappointed, and parental guilt will set in. You know that he will cry and pout through his sibling's activity.

You also told a friend you would help her with wedding planning this Saturday, forgetting all about your children's activity schedule. She is your best friend and the wedding is in three weeks. You are completely overwhelmed and feel victim to your circumstance. It would be nice to have a clone so you can get everything done without losing your mind.

Possible choices:

- Cry, stomp, and yell at your spouse about your circumstances. (Be a victim; do nothing.)

- Try and do it all! Take each child to a portion of their activities and tell your friend you will meet her later in the day. (Urgency wins.)

- Best response: Prioritize what's most important for the day. In this case, your best friend's wedding is a once-in-a-lifetime proposition. The children will have activities for years to come. They will recover from missing one game. Help them understand why they are skipping their activities. It's never too early to teach children about setting priorities in their lives. (Importance wins!)

- Another option: Phone a friend, family member, or coach to share in transporting the children. This will be especially important if the child's activity is of high importance—like a tournament game. (Having a supportive network can diminish the urgency and sometimes facilitate solving the immediate challenge.)

Sometimes when we do not immediately respond to tasks set by others, we can be perceived as apathetic or lazy. More often, it is not because this perception is true but rather because there's a misalignment between parties on the perceived urgency and importance of the task or activity. Be prepared to answer for your actions (or lack thereof) should this situation arise. It is always okay to politely explain that your needs and wants must sometimes take precedence over other people's demands.

> *"He who every morning plans the transactions of that day and follows that plan carries a thread that will guide him through the labyrinth of the most busy life."*
> — Victor Hugo

Breathe

> *"If you want to conquer the anxiety of life, live in the moment, live in the breath."*
> — Amit Ray

My head is pounding after running the length of a football field to catch my connecting flight. My only "touchdown" however, is finally landing in my seat, after fighting for the last space in the overhead bin for luggage and retaining the presence of mind not to say something unladylike to the person in the aisle who keeps hitting my arm with their backpack.

How did I lose so much time? If only I had said no to that last meeting, I would never have been this rushed getting to the airport. Unfortunately, I caved in to *their perceived crisis*, which turned out to be something I could have dealt with over the phone or in an e-mail. I tell myself, *BREATHE!* Wait…do I even know what that means?

How many times have I said that word to myself and did nothing or took one deep breath and blew it out while expecting my current circumstance to immediately fix itself? How many times have I closed my eyes and prayed that by the time I opened them, I would have been magically transported to another place without so much craziness? Unfortunately, neither solution has worked for me in the past. However, with some refined skills in purposeful breathing, it could.

Since breathing is something we can control and regulate, it is a useful tool for achieving a relaxed and clear state of mind. There are many practitioners who teach a variety of breathing techniques worldwide. Many are grounded in the arts of meditation, tai chi, and yoga. The commonality across all these techniques is the ability of the participant to focus and let go one moment at a time. You may want to try several techniques to see which one works for you.

Harvard Health Publications encourages practicing breath focus. Breath focus helps you concentrate on slow, deep breathing and aids you in disengaging from distracting thoughts and sensations. They describe the process below:

Find a quiet, comfortable place to sit or lie down. Close your eyes. First, take a normal breath. Then try a deep breath: Breathe in slowly through your nose, allowing your chest and lower belly to rise as you fill your lungs. Let your abdomen expand fully. Now breathe out slowly through your mouth (or your nose, if that feels more natural).

To assist in relaxation, pick a focus word or short phrase to repeat; relax your muscles as you breathe slowly and naturally; as you exhale, repeat your focus word; continue for at least 2-3 minutes repeating the focus word (up to 20 minutes if you have time). When done, keep your eyes closed as you allow other thoughts to return to your mind. Open your eyes.[3]

Some of us go straight to our "happy place"—that special place where, upon closing our eyes, we can visualize peace and joy. Going there in our minds offers us immediate release from the stresses in front of us. It could be that quiet beach you love, or memories of hiking in the mountains, or a place you want to be (even though the experience is only in your mind). There is a body of work that refers to this type of visualization as entering a state of *mindfulness* (a state of *being*, not *doing*).

Drew Hansen, in an article in *Forbes* titled "A Guide to Mindfulness at Work," describes "mindfulness" as moment-to-moment awareness. Although it originated in the Buddhist tradition, one doesn't have to be Buddhist to reap its benefits. This description explains the basic philosophy:

When you are mindful...You become keenly aware of yourself and your surroundings, but you simply observe these things as they are. You are aware of your own thoughts and feelings, but you do not react to them in the way that you would if you were on "autopilot"...By not labeling or judging the events and circumstances taking place around you, you are freed from your normal tendency to react to them.

Here are a few simple techniques that you can incorporate every day, even at work:

- *Spend at least five minutes each day doing nothing*

- *Get in touch with your senses by noticing the temperature of your skin and background sounds around you*

- *Pay attention to your walking by slowing your pace and feeling the ground against your feet*[4]

A number of well-known companies have integrated the practice of mindfulness programs for their employees. It has become an integral part of their corporate culture. Many have linked these practices (i.e., three minutes of focused breathing at the start of a business meeting) with increased productivity up to 32 percent. It is likely that these employees feel not only more mindful while at work, but they also feel appreciated and valued by their employers. Some of these companies include:

- Apple
- Google
- McKinsey & Company
- Procter & Gamble
- General Mills
- Aetna[5]

The *New York Times* featured Google in an article titled "O.K., Google, Take a Deep Breath." Employees coming from fast-paced fields, already accustomed to demanding bosses and long hours, say Google pushes them to produce at a pace even faster than they could have imagined. Google's co-founder and chief executive, Larry Page, promised on the company website to maintain "a healthy disregard for the impossible." So Google began to offer hundreds of free classes to their employees related to mindfulness. The classes have three steps: attention training, self-knowledge and self-mastery, and the creation of useful mental habits. More than 1,000 employees have taken the class and it always has a waiting list each year.[6]

The theory behind mindfulness is that by increasing focus and self-awareness, we reduce stress, lower blood pressure, improve our memory, and decrease anxiety and depression…an all-around WIN for body, mind, and spirit! More good news is that the practices of focused breathing and mindfulness can be done in just minutes. How can we afford *not* to do this?

> *"Sometimes it's the same moments that take your breath away that breathe purpose and love back into your life."*
> — Steve Maraboli

Drop the "I"

> *"Turn off your e-mail; turn off your phone; disconnect from the Internet; figure out a way to set limits so you can concentrate when you need to, and disengage when you need to. Technology is a good servant but a bad master."*
> —Gretchen Rubin

The Internet is an essential tool for most people today, but there are still those who do not realize how much time they waste online. Managing Internet time usage is a great improvement to your lifestyle. Not only does it help you become more effective in your daily living, but it can also improve your productivity as a whole. By effectively managing the time you spend on the Internet, you can allot more time to focus on the important aspects of life.

Ask yourself why you are using the Internet. If you are using it for work purposes, like doing research, making reports, performing write-ups, or writing articles, then your Internet use is, in fact, essential. But, if you are parked in front of the computer only to keep yourself updated with the latest "news" on social networking sites or combating boredom with online gaming, then you are just wasting your time and should re-think your daily activities.

If you cannot detach from using the Internet, you may actually have an addiction and need help to detach. Science has already established that early or excessive use of screens and digital devices affects us neurologically—some people more than others. It's different for everyone, and you need to understand that your "wiring" is unique to you.

The signs of tech and Internet dependence or addiction include obsessive or compulsive gaming, social media, or Internet activity; and heightened restlessness, irritability, anger, anxiety, or withdrawal when access to it is limited or denied.

A person more vulnerable to Internet dependence may also use gaming or excessive time on the Internet or social media as a coping mechanism, for instance, to deal with emotional turbulence or social anxiety and to satisfy unfulfilled psychological needs.

Steiner-Adair and Barker, in their book, *The Big Disconnect: Protecting Childhood and Family Relationships in the Digital Age*, state:

We love our tech—our smartphones, tablets, social media, and the Internet—and increasingly more of us are confronting the hard truth: that we love it too much. About 16 percent of 18- to 25-year-olds are involved in compulsive Internet use. Some of us could feel powerless in our relationship with it. But addiction?

Although Internet addiction is not formally recognized in the United States as a mental illness, there is a growing concern among medical practitioners and health officials who see the need to offer therapy and treatment centers for it, and treat the phenomenon as something more complicated than simply a social problem. Beneath it all is the deeper damage that tech and Internet dependence can cause. Excessive use can become a source of chronic tension, compromised physical health, emotional distress, decreased performance at work and school, and an obstacle to emotional intimacy.[7]

You really don't know how far over the edge you have gone, until you disconnect by force or by choice. I have experienced this personally on several occasions. There is always the initial anxiety over what you will miss during the downtime or separation from the "I." Then, as more time passes, you relax and revert to simpler times of talking and listening to the people around you. Here are some options to consider to help you drop the "I":

Go into cruise mode. Decide to detach from your phones and Internet for at least 5-10 days, as if you were going on a cruise out of the country. Most of us turn off the phones and Internet on a cruise to escape the enormous fees for minutes of air time at sea. Even though the stress of letting go may be high that first day, by day two we usually have a whole new perspective— focusing on the beauty around us and that fabulous buffet line! The world doesn't come to an end during our down time and we use our minutes in a more valuable way for our mind, body, and spirit. Why can't we do this on land? Sometimes we should all take an extended vacation from the

"I" to remember how easily we once functioned without it. The benefits may astound you.

Give yourself a curfew. Resolve to shut off access to your phones and Internet at a certain hour each day. You may decide to give yourself a different curfew on weekends. The point is, cut yourself off and stick to it. Tell your friends and family so they are aware of your restrictions. Use the minutes you gain on other identified priorities in your life—including yourself and those you love! I actually offered this option as a *Drop the I* challenge on Facebook. You can only imagine the amount of excuses and resistance. I believe I got one participant after posting for over a week. Start small when you begin your technology diet. Even an hour before bedtime gives you back 60 minutes of your life. What will you do with that extra 60 minutes?

Commit to full attention during meetings. Decide to put away all your "I"s during meetings to offer the speaker your full attention. Remember, when we are distracted, our ability to actually hear and understand the information being transmitted lessens significantly. Most meetings average an hour in length. Are we really so indispensable that we cannot detach for an hour without tragic results? And what a waste of time it is to spend an hour in a meeting only to forget what all we heard. You can absolutely survive without your phone and the Internet during all types of face-to-face meetings. This level of commitment can even extend into your personal life— like restricting phone use at dinner. Now, what ever will we talk about over the appetizer?

Quit social media cold turkey. Decide to walk away from social media. As much as Facebook, Twitter, and Instagram have given us immediate peeks into each other's lives, they also act like intoxicating drugs. Repeat engagement with these Internet platforms leaves us wanting more, and then feeling unsatisfied once we get it. Some people go online daily to check for new information or postings. Others stay connected almost minute by minute, leaving the apps open at work and home for quick access. Is that level of connectedness really imperative? What valuable minutes are you trading in exchange for time on social media? Or is this your version of reality TV? You truly don't need that much interaction in your friends' virtual lives. Step away from the keyboard!

Get help! Acknowledge that you need help to disconnect or minimize your compulsion for the "I." Seek out a friend or family member, local support group, or psychologist to assist you in the process. It may be just what you need to take back control of this part of your life.

Notice that each option requires you to make the decision to proceed. The choice is up to you. How many "hot minutes" do you want to get back in your life?

Just Say No

"Let today mark a new beginning for you. Give yourself permission to say NO without feeling guilty, mean, or selfish. Anybody who gets upset and/or expects you to say YES all of the time clearly doesn't have your best interest at heart. Always remember: You have a right

to say NO without having to explain yourself.
Be at peace with your decisions."
— Stephanie Lahart

How many lost minutes have we banked by saying yes to something when we really want to say *NO*? As a former CEO of a health system, I felt I needed to say yes to every chicken dinner I was invited to. I had so much chicken on the East Coast and salmon on the West Coast that I thought I would either sprout wings or fins. Somehow, I told myself that this is what all CEOs did and so there I sat, going from one charity function to the next, one board dinner to the next, one community meeting to the next...just trying to do the right thing. The rising numbers on my scale and the minutes lost by attending all of these functions began to add up. Would anyone have thought badly of me if I missed a few? Probably not.

Why Is Just Saying No So Hard?

Quick survey responses from social media (Facebook):

- *In business, because someone else might say "yes" and we may miss that one opportunity.*

- *Because if I know I can, I will. It's who I am. And "no" is so final. (And sometimes I feel guilty if I don't...and I'm not sure why.)*

- *I think it is all about pride. When we say no, some people see themselves as weak. If we can do everything, then we are strong!*

- *I'm a people pleaser so me saying no means I've let them down or disappointed them even if it means I have to go out of my way.*

- *Saying "no" for me is so hard to do because I don't want to disappoint or let anyone down!!*

For the most part, we are a conflict avoidance culture. We will dodge saying no by any means necessary. We don't answer phone calls or e-mails. We avoid those who are asking something of us. We respond passive-aggressively with a *slow yes* to drop the hint that it is really something we do not want to do. But, we don't like giving an honest no. Sometimes, saying no is the most respectful thing you can do for the requester. It actually can save you both time. You get out of having to do something that you didn't want to do. The requester moves on to proposition someone who really wants to participate.

Tips for Saying No

Real Simple recently featured an article titled "10 Guilt-Free Strategies for Saying No." In the article, the author, Amanda Hinnant, offers a scenario in the workplace you may find useful:

Request: *You are offered a promotion that you don't want. Even though it means more money, it demands more hours and more of what your boss calls responsibility and you call tedium.*

What you should say: *"I'm flattered that you want me, but for personal reasons I'm not in a situation where I can take this on. Perhaps in a year from now things will be different. Can we talk again if my circumstances change?"*

Why it works: *If you're caught in this enviable dilemma, your boss will understand you have personal priorities that take precedence.*

Why you shouldn't feel guilty: *By saying no to more time at the office, you're saying yes to other things you cherish, be they long walks alone at sunset or evening time with your children.*

How to avoid the situation in the future: *If a position opens up at your workplace, you could let it be known that you are not in the running. Being forthright saves your manager the trouble of pursuing a candidate who isn't interested.*[8]

This same type of rationales can be used when saying no in your personal life. What about that annual family dinner or church picnic you really didn't want to attend? Say no in a way that doesn't sound like a personal rejection. Respectful truth-telling is always the right way to respond. If you are tired and want some alone time, say so. Many of us wish we had been courageous enough to say no for the same reasons.

Here are some key words you could use to help you just say no:

- No.
- Not at this time.
- No, thank you, I am unable to make it.
- I am sorry, but my plate is so full right now.
- Thanks for thinking of me, but I can't.
- No, thank you, I am learning to limit my commitments.

- No, thank you, but it sounds great.

- If only I had a clone!

- I am so honored, but I can't.

- I just don't have the time it requires.

Saying no in the workplace can be anxiety provoking, as employers are now expecting us to do more in less time. People say yes to these demands because they want to be a team player, look eager, or simply be nice. At work, be sure to think before you respond. Hit the pause button and allow yourself time to evaluate the cost/benefit of saying yes. This could require you to ask for time to consider the request. For example, the cost/benefit ratio is different for a brand new employee trying to prove themselves versus an employee who is burned out and needs to manage their competing priorities.

If you still come to the conclusion that no is the answer, respond in a timely manner and ask if there might be another way you could contribute. In other words, offer an alternative to no. This lets the employer know you understand your limits, but also care about the task at hand and the company (a great characteristic for a leader). And, don't say no over e-mail. Be courageous and give your response in person. Let the requester see your heart through your eyes. Beware of saying too much during this meeting, though. Don't leave your entire calendar up for discussion—just the request in front of you.

What happens if your employer still wants you to proceed, after you have said no? Be ready to lay out current priorities and the time commitment for each. Then ask for help creating a healthy balance so that you can be successful for the good of the company, even if it means incorporating this new task.

Your employer may not be fully aware of the impact the new task has on your current work. Ask how much time you have to complete the request given your current priorities.

Take a more proactive approach at work. During monthly meetings with your supervisor, be sure there is always a review of "what's on your plate" and align priorities for the upcoming quarter. This will offer a better understanding about what time you have to give and avoid the need for the dreaded no.

"I feel because at our core we have a need to feel valued and often times we equate our performance with value. I think about Mary and Martha. Martha saw the things that needed to be done and equated her performance to being loved and valued by Jesus. While Mary understood the value of quality vs. quantity. I have learned through the years some of my most meaningful work comes after I have valued others and myself and said no because I was able to provide better physically, emotionally, and spiritually to what I said yes to. Those we say yes to deserve our very best, not a piece of our best."

— Jacqueline Camp

Hold My Hand: The Role of Collaboration

"Sometimes, reaching out and taking some-one's hand is the beginning of a journey. At other times, it is allowing another to take yours."

— Vera Nazarian

April is a newly appointed leader at a growing medical practice. She has primarily worked independently in past jobs, so leading a team of 20 professionals is a new experience. The clinic offers many challenges in her first few months, with minimal time to waste "fixing" key operational issues. April is determined to be the best leader possible and pushes forward, taking on these tasks alone. She believes she can get them done in a more timely manner rather than involving the other people on her team. She knows training and support would be required and that the training process would only prolong the "fix."

How often in our personal and professional lives do we subscribe to April's approach—just doing a task ourselves instead of involving others? We rationalize our decision as saving *time* for ourselves and possibly our employer, but at what price? Should we really add to our already overloaded plate, which makes us more stressed, or bring in other people on our team to spread out the work and responsibility?

As leaders, we assume that leading means doing it all. For many of us, fear of failure and embarrassment have us clinging to the idea of control. As a result, we often take on more than we should, step on toes, and micromanage without meaning to.

We have to think about collaboration and *time* differently. Collaboration is what occurs when individuals or groups work together, combining their strengths and negating weaknesses to accomplish a set of goals.

Not everything we do collaboratively will offer an immediate time-saving benefit, but sometimes these actions pay off later. For example, collaborating with others on our team is an investment for future savings. Furthermore, when more than one person is skilled to complete the desired task, efficiency will eventually be the result. However, it will take time to train employees to assure proficiency in the tasks at hand. A side benefit of collaboration is the mutual ownership of the results achieved when the team is engaged together.

Collaboration also allows others to bear the workload. For instance, when dealing with a new project, the work becomes a series of problems you need to solve. Tapping into the distributed intelligence of a group increases your chances of solving problems more efficiently. Communication between team members increases, which will improve your future collaborations as well.

Many corporate cultures and leaders throughout the country are shifting from an outdated directive approach toward collaborative frameworks that inspire us to engage in new and different ways with our work and with each other.

When thinking about collaboration, some key steps to successful implementation that will reap benefits in time savings include:

- **Identify the right partners.** Different tasks require different partnerships. Are you looking for a group to vet new ideas (open collaboration), or to complete a focused project, or do you require ownership across multiple stakeholders?

- **Make sure all participants are willing/ready to participate.** If time is an issue, dealing with a naysayer will only prolong the task.

- **Clarify roles and responsibilities of each team player.** Time is wasted when people are not clear on what they are to do and why.

- **Good facilitation of group process will be essential.** Collaboration does not mean you proceed in a free for all without a leader. "Group think" requires someone to guide the work, reflect agreed-upon commitments, chart progress to date, and cheer on success.

- **Don't underestimate the time it will take to build the team able to achieve efficiency and sustainable results.** Building consistency and proficiency takes time, and people need to be prepared to be in it for the long haul. Keep reminding yourself that the benefits will outweigh implementation time.

"If two heads are better than one, then what about double chins? On that note, I will help myself to seconds."

— Jarod Kintz

Stop Owning Other Folks' Stuff!

"Chances are if you find yourself caught up in a political foofaraw at work, or in some family squabble at home, it's because someone else is succeeding in convincing you that his problem is your problem. The non-self-destructor recognizes this and as soon as possible, gives the sleepless night back to the person to whom it belongs."

— Jason Seiden

Have you ever said, "Never mind…I will do it myself"? In our haste to get something done—or out of sheer frustration—we often take on the additional work of others even though we may be stretched to the limit. We may think this is a time saver, and it very well could be in the short run. However, mark my words: The person truly responsible for the task in question will take your precious minutes from you again and again. They will drag their feet on future tasks, knowing that you will always say, "Never mind."

All parents reading this book should be able to relate to this concept. Our children play this game with us all the time. Have you ever noticed how long your children take to complete their chores? In many cases, they are hoping we get so frustrated that we just do it ourselves. The reason for their behavior should not always be labeled "laziness" though. In some cases, it could be related to a perceived value of the child or even the family. We all tend to be more willing to engage in activities that we value. Their inaction could even be related to lack of skills needed to complete the task.

A related scenario often plays out at work. Lower performing employees or those who are disengaged from their work use the dragging feet phenomenon as an effective tactic to do less. They even tend to seek out the "never minder" coworker or leader in order to get them to do their work for them. Most people know the "never minders" in the organization, the same way children know which parent will eventually give in.

Here's the short tip for gaining back your minutes: STOP OWNING OTHER FOLKS' STUFF! Hold those around you—even your children—accountable for their responsibilities. They need to value their minutes and respect yours! Don't let "never mind" be the rule, but the exception. Don't be fooled into thinking owning other folks' stuff will somehow gain you more time. It actually sucks the life out of you on so many levels.

We have a saying at Studer Group®, a Huron Healthcare solution: "What gets rewarded gets repeated." In this case, by saying, "Never mind," we are rewarding a negative behavior that needs to stop.

We also lose some of our hot minutes owning the emotional issues of others. How many minutes are wasted worrying about those we love to the point of making ourselves physically and emotionally ill?

This is definitely a personal struggle for me. I understand the desire to do this for our children, but what about the adults in our lives who have made grown-up decisions that placed them in their current situations? How do you find the balance between caring and taking on an unhealthy burden?

The answer is to let your loved ones know that you support them, but that you won't get wrapped up in their drama. Ask them to respect your boundaries and be adamant when you decide that you have to step back from their "stuff."

Spiritual leader Ian Lawton, in an online blog, "10 Ways to Know You Are Taking Too Much Responsibility," describes the following indicators of "responsibility imbalance":

- *You need to fill conversational silences.*

- *You apologize for things you had nothing to do with.*

- *You take on the blame for events and circumstances that are beyond your control.*

- *You make excuses for people who are behaving badly.*

- *Your first inkling is to rescue people.*

- *You feel paralyzed by the size of challenges.*

- *You lose sleep, worrying about world problems.*

- *You feel like you always have to be the life of the party.*

- *You deprive yourself of basic rights because others are missing out.*

- *You struggle with guilt.*[9]

If you identify with any of these descriptors, you may want to have a long talk with yourself about how much of yourself and your time you sacrifice for other folks' stuff. Learn to allow them all to accept responsibility for their own lives and figure out a way to accept where they "are." Then return those un-used hot minutes back to your emotional bank account.

Live Your Minutes Purposefully

"If you want to identify me, ask me not where I live, or what I like to eat, or how I comb my hair, but ask me what I think I am living for, in detail, and ask me what I think is keeping me from living fully for the thing I want to live for."

— Thomas Merton

Living purposefully doesn't mean doing something just because someone else tells you it's important and purposeful. Instead, it means doing what brings you a sense of pleasure and fulfillment. The more you can find fulfillment in what you do each day, the more you can contribute to the world by being who you are and living with purpose.

If you are giving a lot and receiving little in return in terms of your own happiness, that's a clear sign that you need to reevaluate how you're spending your time and who you are spending it with. And, if you choose to spend your time doing what gives you a sense of fulfillment, it doesn't mean that you care any less about your relationships. It does mean however, that you value your time above all and make it a priority.

This notion of purposeful minutes hit home for me over the last several years during the prolonged illness and eventual death of my father. We lived in North Carolina, and my parents lived in Maryland. The distance of a six-hour commute kept me from visiting home as often as I would have liked and spending time with my father.

I knew his condition was deteriorating with each visit, so I needed to make sure the time we spent together was special. I valued each precious minute when he smiled or laughed at little things. His smile would light up the room whenever the grandchildren were around. Although he was quite miserable, near the end of his life, I valued those minutes as well, just "being" with him. I wanted to remember everything. I never felt like any of my time spent with him was wasted. It was important and purposeful, even if it was about saying goodbye.

As I said my last goodbye at his funeral, I kept wishing for more purposeful minutes with him. My mind was flooded with images from my childhood. I remember sitting at the dinner table after all homework was done and listening to him tell stories about "back in the day." I was about 15 years old. I knew some of his stories were embellished and grand, but that didn't matter. In those precious minutes before bed, we escaped to a special place. I was his princess, and he was my hero.

The experiences with my father made me realize that if we look too far down the road, always planning and worrying about things that have yet to happen, we sometimes miss the value of what is *here and now*. Why do we wait until the end of life or tragic experiences with those we love (i.e., like sickness or injury) to realize the value of purposeful minutes in our relationships each day? Why do we put off taking back just a few minutes for personal fulfillment?

It doesn't take much effort to move toward a more purposeful life. Start with a few things that "fill your cup" and bring you joy. And begin to eliminate the things that are time consuming and offer very little or no return. Those activities usually drain your energy and divert you from things that are (or should be) a higher priority in the scope of your life.

Some people may find this shift difficult. We do so many things out of habit or to fulfill other people's expectations. So it feels funny when we change our usual pattern of behavior. We make all kinds of excuses as to why we can't do something different or new. Try just one small change at a time and soon you will be on your way to dropping your time robbers and adding more activities that fill your cup. Some of your new activities may actually offer you increased energy. This is often the case when we spend our time doing something that we love.

A good example for me is my love for dance. I started doing Zumba about four years ago. At the time, I was looking for a group of women I could relax and have fun with while burning a few calories (okay, a lot of calories!). From the moment I started, I was in love. Not just because of the incredible friendships I have gained, but because of my true love for dance.

When I dance, my mind is completely free. All I feel is the music. I go to a serene place where there is no worry, no stress, no complexity…just inner peace.

In the beginning, I didn't know how I would fit this new love into my crazy life and work schedule. Then, I made a conscious decision to schedule it on my calendar and make it a priority just like any other business meeting. I even told my assistant not to schedule meetings or conference calls during that time because it was important to me. It's one hour, three or four times a week. Zumba has gone from being an optional activity to an integral part of my life that makes me whole. And, my energy level has dramatically improved. Today, I am a licensed Zumba instructor!

Some people have a clear vision of what makes up their purposeful minutes—as if the path was laid out for them and they simply need to take the first step. For others, the vision is unclear and the path elusive. They may not have given it a single thought as they race through life.

Here are some things to consider as you chart your path:

- **Remember.** Think back to all the times you've felt fulfilled in life. You could even go all the way back to your childhood. Then ask yourself these questions: *What was I doing? Who was I with? What emotions was I feeling? Did I have moments when I lost track of time because I was doing something I loved?*

- **Change your perspective.** Instead of asking, *What is my purpose?* try asking, *Who is the person I am trying to become?* Changing the question can help shift your perspective and open yourself up to an abundance of creative ideas and experiences you may have never thought possible.

- **Take action!** What are you waiting for? Get out of your own way. Precious minutes are passing you by.

Every moment of those 525,600 minutes we get each year matters. Let's make every minute meaningful, thoughtful, and purposeful. Don't look back and think, *I should have...*

Laugh

Have you ever noticed that when you are in a bad mood, the day seems to drag on forever? At the end of the day, you don't feel like you got much done and you chalk up the day as a loss. But when your day is filled with joy and laughter, it seems like you are full of energy and knocking out your "to-do" list at warped speed.

When you laugh, you get a release of endorphins, giving you a "feel good" factor. The whole body relaxes and stress and tension are reduced. Plus, your laughter has a positive impact on others around you because laughter is contagious and helps lift everyone's mood.

Laughter can be a powerful motivator. It can build cohesion during a team project, make a task seem less daunting, and improve productivity. Laughter connects people easily with each other. It helps to develop a positive mental attitude, optimism, and increases communication skills.

Not everything in our day is so serious that we can't use laughter as an appropriate tool to promote wellness in the workplace and at home. This is not about laughing *at* people, but *with* the people around you to improve the quality of your personal and professional lives. What a great way to spend your minutes!

I realize that it can be difficult to objectively judge how you spend your own time. Learning how to step back and assess the things you put your energy toward each day is a valuable skill—and skills like this can take some practice before they are mastered. It is vitally important to pay attention to the choices you make each day, and this chapter has given you some tools to help you take that necessary closer look. This level of self-assessment is *the way* you become aware of the activities that repeatedly waste your precious minutes.

When you pay attention to how much time you spend online, the minutes you let slip by mindlessly watching television, or the countless hours you waste worrying over various problems instead of taking action, you will start to see your patterns of wastefulness emerge in technicolor. And as the saying goes, once you know better, you can do better. By learning to maximize your minutes, you can start living your newly authentic, purposeful, and joyous life.

"It doesn't matter what you did or where you were…it matters where you are and what you're doing. Get out there! Sing the song in your heart and NEVER let anyone shut you up!!"

— Steve Maraboli

CHAPTER FOUR:

What Can You Do In...? (Small Blocks of Hot Minutes Really Add Up!)

Successful time management happens on a daily basis. So it makes sense to break your day into blocks of manageable time and develop achievable goals for each day. Whether it's a task you need to complete at work, an assignment you must finish for school, or a list of chores around the house, you can get it all done by making the most of all of your hot minutes.

First, wake up and decide which goals you want to achieve today. Estimate how long it will take you in minutes, leaving a few extra minutes for the unexpected. Schedule your day so that your number-one goal receives the majority of your time. Don't procrastinate by tackling the unimportant tasks or tasks that could be accomplished on another day.

It is also important to know your own productivity rhythm. If you are a morning person, be sure to schedule the most important task of the day in the morning. If you work best in the evening, save the most important task until then. The idea is to match your goals with the time that you can achieve peak (and the most efficient) performance. And try and stick to your own schedules so that you can control the pace of the day.

Many of us throw away potentially useful blocks of time surfing the Internet, staring mindlessly at the TV, or just sitting spaced out and bored in a traffic jam. Of course, there is a time and place for doing nothing. Human beings aren't meant to always be productive, and they probably couldn't be if they tried. However, there are times we'd be better served to make those "chill" minutes into "hot" ones.

Making the Most of Your Hot Minutes

1-5 Minutes: The BEST Use of Those "Throwaway" Moments

Out of the 1,440 minutes ticking by in a day, we can *all* find five minutes in which to achieve a few small goals. We have five minutes between meetings or phone calls. We have five minutes standing in a line or waiting for our lunch to arrive. We check our e-mail, idly surf the web, or check out apps on our phones. We tweet or do a Facebook update. Or we sit and wait.

Many times, those five minutes just pass us by and we are no closer to our goals than we were before—and once they're gone, they're *gone*. In a very real sense we threw them away. What a waste! And at the end of the day, we wonder where the day went.

Our days are made up of all of those five-minute choices.

Let's start really small with a One-Minute Rule. Remember the old rule we used when trying to justify not throwing away food that had accidentally fallen on the floor? If it was on the surface for only five seconds, then we went ahead and ate it anyway. We truly believed that the *time* of contact changed the outcome.

I would like to propose adopting that same concept, except in this case we extend the *time* to one minute. And instead of impacting what we eat, we will aim for the BEST* outcome when we believe we are out of control. Here's what I mean by BEST:

- **B**reathe to slow your thoughts. (10 seconds)

- **E**valuate the choices. (20 seconds)

- **S**elect top three priorities. (20 seconds)

- **T**ake action. (10 seconds)

* This exercise requires the awareness that you are out of control or overwhelmed and want to be proactive in changing direction and getting control over your day. This will not work if you are a victim to your busyness.

Many of us use the saying, "If I only had five minutes..." Here are some things you can do in just five minutes:

- Review your schedule.

- Return 3-5 e-mails.

- Write in your journal.

- Listen to an inspiring song (or sing it to yourself).

- Take a stretch break.

- Organize your workspace (unless it's way out of control, requiring a lot more time).

- Pause. Look out of a window and enjoy your surroundings.

- Tell someone thank you or offer a compliment.

15-30 Minutes: A "Break" That Makes a Real Impact

If each of us had to use a time clock to punch in the minutes of our lives, we would probably rethink how we used them—especially if we got paid for only those minutes that added value to our lives. On a subconscious level, we parcel our time in 15- or 30-minute intervals. This includes things like: planned breaks (15 minutes), meetings (30 minutes), and meal times (30 minutes). Employers even break work time into 15- and 30-minute intervals.

Understanding what you can do with small increments of time that can add value lies in self-reflection. You will need to take the time to figure out how long it takes you to complete routine tasks in your life. We are not all the same; therefore we work and produce at different rates.

To help you prioritize the important things and maximize how you use your minutes, see the section titled "Reflect, Prioritize, Act" in Chapter 3. Remember to:

- Journal how you usually spend your time in 24 hours. Be honest. Your self-assessment should not reflect what you wish it to be but actually how you spend your time.

- Plan to spend at least 50 percent of your time engaged in the thoughts, activities, and conversations that offer you the most value or yield the greatest results. Discern between activities that are important versus urgent. Put those higher priority tasks on your daily to-do list.

- Compare your current schedule with your priorities. If there is a misalignment, make adjustments to maximize how you use your minutes. This forces you to get rid of those activities that are purely a waste of time.

In 15-30 minutes you could:

- Return a call or make a call to connect with a loved one.
- Clear your inbox of e-mail clutter.
- Read your child a book.
- Exercise (i.e., take a walk, ride your bike).
- Clean a room in your house.
- Cook a quick meal.
- Pay a few bills online.

60 Minutes-12 Hours: A Massive Window of Opportunity

Sixty minutes or more can truly be classified as "hot minutes," primarily because of the larger personal commitment involved in how they are spent. In other words, they can either add value to your life or they can vanish unused, in a flash. But if you strive to stay present, in even one hour's time, you can get a tremendous amount of things done. Imagine the potential in spending several focused hours working toward your to-do list. You are practically unstoppable when you work with time in this manner.

Set your watch, phone, or computer to ring every hour. When you hear the ring, take a deep breath and ask yourself if you spent your last hour productively. Then look at your calendar and deliberately recommit to how you are going to efficiently use the next hour. Don't let the hours manage you! When you manage your day hour by hour using this technique, you will be amazed to see how much more you can get done.

In 60 minutes you could:

- Spend quality time with family or friends.
- Read the newspaper or catch up on social media.
- Complete a doctor/dental appointment.
- Attend a business meeting.
- Write a report.
- Watch your favorite TV show.
- Complete a workout at home or your favorite gym.

In 4 hours you could:

- Go to the movies.
- Go shopping for fun or essentials.
- Read a book.
- Get a spa treatment.
- Play a round of golf.
- Volunteer at your favorite charity.
- Cook dinner or bake your favorite treats.
- Practice Zumba routines.
- Finish the laundry.

In 12 hours you could:

- Take a day trip with family or friends to the beach or mountains.

- Participate in a marathon (less time if you are fast).

- Paint a couple of rooms in your house.

- Get caught up on your to-do list.

- Attend a strategic planning session for work.

- Attend a conference for professional growth.

Notice that these suggestions aren't always "all business." Some (many, in fact) are about personal renewal or just plain having fun. The point is to use your hot minutes mindfully— *choosing* how to spend your precious time rather than letting it slip away unnoticed, unfulfilled, and unappreciated.

Make Sleep a Priority!

You must schedule sleep like any other daily activity, so put it on your to-do list and cross it off every night. But don't make it the thing you do only after everything else is done. Schedule a stopping point in your day so you can get the sleep you need. Remember that if you are not rested, your productivity will suffer. Plus, you just won't feel as great as you should. Aim for at least eight hours of quality sleep each night. Here are some tips to help you achieve restorative sleep:

- Stick to a sleep schedule, even on weekends.

- Practice a relaxing bedtime ritual. Books, music, and a partner massage all calm the mind and prepare the body for sleep.

- Exercise daily. Be careful not to exercise too late in the day. It could actually have the opposite effect and keep you awake. Exercise paired with a hot shower or bath may be the perfect one-two punch needed to knock you out for the night!

- Evaluate your bedroom to ensure ideal temperature, sound, and light. Room darkening shades are highly effective.

- Sleep on a comfortable mattress and good quality pillows.

- Beware of hidden "sleep robbers" like alcohol and caffeine.

- Turn off electronics before bed. Sleeping with the TV on can prevent you from getting a sound sleep.

What all would be on your list of things you could accomplish in five minutes or over the course of several hours? Even if you have only a single minute a day, practice the BEST technique to put you back on track and motivate you to keep going. Make optimizing your precious minutes a part of your daily routine. By controlling what you can in manageable segments, you are sure to waste fewer minutes, hours, and days...which add up to weeks, months, and years.

CHAPTER FIVE:

But, I'm the Boss! How to Take Charge of Your Time When You're in Charge of EVERYTHING

"Don't be fooled by the calendar. There are only as many days in the year as you make use of. One man gets only a week's value out of a year while another man gets a full year's value out of a week."

—Charles Richards

Tick, tock; tick, tock…will this clock ever stop long enough for me to get everything done today?

How many times have you had this thought? You don't have to be a leader to experience the stress, anxiety, and unhappiness that come from feeling like your life is out of control. From time to time we all feel this way. Yet even more than most, leaders—in particular, female leaders—may feel crushed by all the demands on their time.

First, let's look at some of the challenges women face. The typical day for a woman in leadership will probably never mirror that of her male counterpart. There are often other roles for women to fill that don't have a paycheck attached to them and that aren't part of a five-year career plan. In addition to their professional responsibilities, women are often wives, mothers, housekeepers, chefs, repairpersons, bus drivers, disciplinarians, master schedulers, and more; in other words, the nuclei for their entire families. Success in business means that women have to find a way to balance all these roles. For example, current societal expectations in the workplace are rarely flexible or accommodating to working moms...so that forces women to choose between their children and their careers. Add in the expectations or norms for people in leadership (like working 12- to14-hour days) and this balancing act becomes even more challenging.

Regardless of whether leaders are female or male, there are other reasons why they might feel stressed by time constraints. For one thing, leadership positions are especially challenging because you are responsible not only for your own work, but also for the productivity and achievements of all the people working beneath you. Talk about a high-stress position! You may have additional tasks that take up extra time before, during, and after work, such as planning and leading meetings, implementing system-wide changes, developing new ideas, or heading up brainstorming sessions.

And of course, there are those mundane activities that we can't do anything about. We all have to wait in lines, at red lights, for elevators, and so on. So what are savvy leaders today supposed to do to better manage their time? For starters, we must start making better choices and learn to "just say no."

The first step is to figure out *where your time is currently going!* If you want to make improvements, you've got to first know what to improve. To find the answer, I suggest you track your time for two weeks so you can make some educated decisions about which areas you need to improve. It turns out that much of our time is often taken up by "how we do things" or isn't spent wisely because we lose focus on the most important priorities (main things).

I encourage you to remember what a dear mentor, Quint Studer, told me early in my tenure working for Studer Group®: "80 percent of your results will come from 20 percent of your activities." It's your responsibility to yourself and your team to know where your highest payoff activities are and to try to eliminate as many low payoff activities as you can.

Now classify your activities. Are you actually engaging in activities that offer a high payoff (in other words, focusing on what's most important), and if so, how well are you doing them? I urge you to sit down and spend at least 30 minutes honestly assessing your performance. You don't have to limit your self-assessment to just leadership or work-related activities. Think about activities that impact your life outside of work, too. Do they offer you a "high payoff" or added value?

While each person—and therefore each person's schedule—is unique, most leaders can make certain types of changes that will lead to major improvements. This chapter will explore leadership time robbers and how smart leaders can reclaim some of their "hot minutes."

Time Robbers for Leaders

It's 7:30 a.m. Exactly 30 minutes before my first meeting of the day. That's just enough time to check a few e-mails, grab a cup of coffee, and take a few deep breaths to center my mind. As I make my way down the hall, I see one of my employees pacing outside my office door (never a good sign at this time of day). Oh no, this was not on my calendar! Please, no drama to start my day. I have no time…no minutes to spare.

This scenario probably sounds very familiar to most leaders. Employees requiring our immediate attention can derail the best-laid schedule or most thoughtfully constructed to-do list. We never build in minutes for unanticipated interruptions and often schedule our days so tightly that even restroom breaks are a challenge.

There never seems to be enough time to address the demands of leadership, which results in frustration, decreased quality of work, and diminished efficiency. Being "all things to all people" on demand is not in any leadership job description, yet, we step into those shoes more often than not. We equate quantity of time on the clock with the quality of our leadership and wonder why this stance has not served us well.

The truth is, leaders who effectively manage the time robbers in their lives operate at a higher level of functioning and drive their organizations to a higher level of performance. They also serve as great role models for the staff in what "right" looks like.

The following are examples of some of the biggest time robbers for leaders:

- **Managing roadblocks.** Unanticipated organizational change that is external (i.e., economic pressures, governmental mandates) or internal (i.e., structural, functional) can be all-consuming for leaders, requiring reprioritization of goals, action plans, and time.

- **Indecision.** Failure to take action.

- **Implementation before diagnosis.** Taking action before figuring out the underlying issues that inform the direction our actions should take.

- **Unanticipated interruptions.** Disruptions that redirect our time and cause us to lose focus.

- **Procrastination.** Time wasted avoiding a task or project.

- **Unrealistic time estimates.** Actions/projects require more or less time than perceived. These errors usually occur when goal setting and action plans are created in isolation, without input from others on the team. Unrealistic time estimates could also cause employees to rush through a project, creating errors that could have been avoided with more time.

- **Reactive versus proactive leadership.** Always chasing the next organizational "fire" is time consuming and exhausting.

- **Poor organizational skills.**

- **Ineffective communication.** Lack of clarity or effective strategies to assure messages are received as intended.

- **Communicating with difficult employees.** Creates a never-ending drain on your leadership minutes if not managed well. Communication and setting boundaries will be the key to managing this time robber.

- **Ineffective meetings.**

- **Limited delegation.**

- **Limited ability to prioritize for self and organization.**

Maximizing Minutes for the Leader and Staff

Leaders with strong time management and organizational skills are able to demonstrate powerful techniques for their team members, making everyone more productive. Key factors in strong time management are being aware of the vision, setting specific and realistic goals, establishing and communicating priorities, and having the discipline to follow the plan.

In other words, leaders must function like the organization's GPS—the technology we use to get from point A to point B in our cars. Once a direction (vision for the future) has been set by the board of directors, leaders must follow a defined set of instructions (goals) to arrive at the desired destination (results). The more clarity conveyed in the instructions (turn by turn), the faster the arrival time. If we choose to take an alternate route, we may lose a lot of time finding our way or getting back on course. As a leader, how many times have you gone off track or given vague instructions to your staff, only to waste a lot of time "recalculating your route" in order to get the team where you want them to go?

Well-defined goals will outline the work that needs to be done, the timeframe in which it needs to be accomplished, and resources that can maximize results in the shortest time possible. Great goals are SMART: **S**pecific, **M**easurable, **A**chievable, **R**ealistic, and **T**racked over time.

Going back to the GPS analogy, think about a time in which you didn't know the complete address to a desired location and could enter only partial information into the GPS. Without the street name or house number, did your estimated arrival time change? Did you have to stop to ask for directions? Without fail, a lack of clear goals robs you of valuable leadership minutes.

When well-defined goals are coupled with strong action plans, efficiency is propelled to a higher level, and thus maximizes your minutes. Action plans break down the tactical work required to accomplish the goal. They include major and minor activities, allocate resources, provide timelines, and bring to light possible obstacles and redundancies. Action plans provide instant focus for team members on current and upcoming priorities.

Everyone on the team must have a clear understanding of the organization's priorities. Organizational alignment improves efficiency. Even though a concentrated amount of time may initially be spent by the leader communicating the "why," "what," and "how" related to those priorities, less time and frustration is spent on rework due to misalignment.

An effective tool that can improve the communication of roles, responsibilities, and deadlines is an annual calendar of all departmental activities. The annual calendar should include regular tasks and anticipated new projects. This tool clearly marks times during which staff will be exceptionally busy and/or stressed. It can pinpoint the spaces where openings exist for new initiatives, and where work with other teams or departments may run into difficulty.

Common events that may be included on an annual calendar are due dates for the annual report, papers, exhibits, reports to funding agencies, budget reports, grant applications, conferences, meetings, presentations, etc. When this kind of calendar is posted in public areas, it strongly communicates to everyone where current energies need to be applied. Organization-wide alignment saves leadership minutes!

The vision for a well-run organization sets its overall direction and priorities. Goals refine the direction into specific targets. Action plans and annual calendars outline and communicate the work that needs to be done and provide deadlines that further help to define priorities. *However, the best plans are useless if the leader and their team are not disciplined enough to follow them.*

General Rules of Thumb for Maximizing Your Minutes (and Your Staff's Minutes, Too!)

- **Make a master schedule.** Include your weekly meetings, classes, or activities that do not vary. Try to consolidate or group activities to preserve unscheduled chunks of usable time. If you have trouble making this schedule, you are probably trying to do too much. Once you make it, consult it and use it to structure your daily activities.

Do not schedule every moment, though, because over-planning is a time robber too.

- **Set aside some uninterrupted planning time each day.** This may be a difficult discipline for some, but 20 uninterrupted minutes of planning yields the same results as 60 minutes of interrupted time. What a return on your time investment!

- **Get into a routine.** Mindless routines may curb your creativity, but when used properly, they can release time and energy back to you. Choose a time to get a certain task accomplished, such as answering e-mail, working on a project, or completing paperwork, and then stick to it every day.

- **Divide large tasks.** Large tasks should be broken up into a series of small tasks. By creating small, manageable tasks, the entire task will eventually be accomplished. Also, by using a piecemeal approach, you will be able to fit it into your hectic schedule.

- **Set start and stop times.** When arranging start times, also arrange stop times.

- **Keep paper moving!** Throw it away, act upon it, or put it in your reading pile. Shuffling and reshuffling paper from pile to pile with no evaluation or action is a waste of your time.

- **Control your e-mail deliveries.** Do you check your e-mails every five minutes? Stop the madness! Work e-mails into your schedule so that they do not control your day.

- **Keep track of who is interrupting you and why.** Then you can make some informed decisions about how to respond to or address a problem. Even if you cannot eliminate the interruption, you can keep it short. A general rule: The length of the interruption is in direct proportion to the comfort level of the interrupter. Don't let the interrupter sit down and get comfortable in your office. If the interrupter does not get the hint that you are in the middle of something, stand up. It sends a signal that this will be a very short and focused conversation.

- **Schedule one-on-one sessions with your boss.** Using a predetermined agenda keeps the discussion focused and within the hour scheduled. If pre-work was completed and sent ahead for review, even better!

- **Ask your team: "What do I do that wastes your time and hinders your performance?"** Some of their suggestions may surprise you and could save you and your team valuable time.

- **Make meetings productive, but short.** The average person wastes about 31 hours per month in unproductive meetings.[1] Most meetings can be accomplished in half the time it currently takes if everyone is prepared, on time, and focused. Using a standardized agenda with a focus on strategic priorities will help to keep everyone's attention on the "main or important things" and cut down on side discussions.

- **Don't fall into the "perpetually-scheduled-meeting" syndrome.** This occurs when you're having meetings just because they are regularly scheduled. Make sure every meeting is absolutely necessary. Routine meetings are a good time investment only if they fulfill or move forward organizational objectives. Do your standing meetings have a charter that is reviewed periodically to see if they are still relevant? Are the right people in attendance for the objectives you need to address at this point in time?

- **Always begin a meeting by covering the most important items first.** This method assures you accomplish what you need to accomplish and that you don't need to rush through the "main" things.

- **When people show up late, don't recap what you've covered.** When you recap, you are rewarding the tardy person and punishing the people who were on time.

- **Start and end your meetings on time.** Think about it: You waste 30 minutes of productivity by beginning a meeting with 10 people three minutes late.

- **Know when to stop a task, policy, or procedure.** Don't maintain initiatives, policies, or procedures for their historical value only. All work should have a purpose that takes the organization to a higher level of performance. It can't be "because we have always done it this way." That kind of thinking is a waste of everyone's time.

- **Eat well, sleep well, exercise plenty, and goof off.** Take care of yourself so that you have the energy to lead. When you lack the "luster" that comes from living a good life, things take more time to complete.

- **Set aside time for reflection.** Find value in those quiet minutes to self-assess, breathe, and refresh. Clear heads are always more efficient.

Short on Time? Focus in on These Quick-Hit Tactics That Take 10 Minutes or Less

All leaders know what it's like to finish a task and realize that you have less than 15 minutes before the next phone call, meeting, or scheduled project. At first you may assume that you won't be able to get much done in such a short amount of time, but of course that isn't true! And most likely, you can't afford to "waste" even 5 or 10 minutes.

Think about it this way: As leaders, we are constantly asked to do more with fewer resources, so every minute we use wisely adds value. Here are a few high-impact tools and tactics that don't take a lot of time but have a high impact on driving results. Choose one to focus on the next time you have a few spare moments. Better yet, look ahead and proactively fit some of these tactics into the gaps in your daily schedule!

- **Rounding for Outcomes (5-minute interaction).** This tactic was designed by Studer Group and has been executed successfully throughout the country for more than a decade. The goal of rounding on employees is to capture important information to act upon, including reward and recognition and process improvement. Rounding can be one of the most powerful tools in your leadership toolbox. It allows leaders to proactively engage, listen, communicate, build relationships, and support our most important customers—our employees. Remember, quality outcomes are built on relationships! Additionally, the information gathered during rounding can be used for coaching opportunities and to directly drive results. Ultimately, rounding leads to improved employee engagement, which is beneficial for many reasons. For example:

- ○ There is a high correlation between employee engagement results and quality outcomes.

- ○ Employee engagement is also correlated with turnover rates—the lower the engagement, the higher the turnover. (Turnover increases variance in execution and performance.)[2]

- **Holding Employee Huddles (5-10 minutes per day).** Huddles are a powerful team builder and accelerator for consistency in execution. A huddle allows the team to "get on the same page" related to the day's priorities. In just 5-10 minutes, the leader can align the staff to unit/departmental goals, review progress to date, connect to purpose, and reward and recognize accomplishments. The team is reenergized, focused, and ready to go.

Huddles are not done on the fly. They have a designated time, an agenda, a dashboard to reference, and an expectation for all to attend.[3] Use a timer if you need to so these huddles don't turn into staff meetings.

To learn more about Rounding for Outcomes and Employee Huddles, please visit www.studergroup.com.

- **Writing Thank-You Notes (5 minutes or less).** An old-fashioned handwritten thank-you note can go a long way toward building relationships with coworkers. It doesn't take much time to write, and the power of this small gesture can last for years to come if received from one's supervisor. If you don't have time to write a note, use your words in person. A thank-you in any form is better than none at all.

- **Learning Something New (10 minutes or less).** Read an uplifting or educational book or blog post. Keeping your mind agile, your idea bank full, and your information current will always make you a better leader.

- **Making Progress on a Goal (10 minutes or less).** Make a phone call or send an e-mail to further a project (not just a reply to what is in the inbox, but something that will proactively move you toward a goal).

- **Reflecting on Your Day So Far (10 minutes or less).** Ask yourself what you have learned and what you need to adjust. It's never too late to make a not-so-good day better, or to make a good day great!

Managing Roadblocks

Organizations that we at Studer Group serve are undergoing significant change right now. They are learning to thrive in a new environment with greater socioeconomic pressures to provide value versus volume. Consumers have access to more and more information when making choices. And employees want to work for companies that stand out as the best in their field. Being the best requires new or revised work processes to enhance efficiencies and the quality of the outcomes achieved—yet multiple roadblocks may get in the way of success. Recognition of the particular roadblock you face is essential to moving forward and maximizing your leadership minutes. Here are three common roadblocks leaders often encounter, as well as tactics to help you continue moving forward.

Roadblock #1: The Stop Sign

Some roadblocks are truly unalterable. These are circumstances that inhibit performance and that employees are not likely to be able to change: the national economy, the organizational structure, funding and paperwork requirements, etc. These are all factors that affect employee performance and how they spend their time, but are beyond individual or collective control. For example, if a change in organizational structure has you reporting to a different leader, that decision is out of your control. Requirements set by your previous leader may change with the new leader. This could include how your time is spent on aspects of your job, and even the hours you work. You will need to stop and course correct, realigning previously set priorities—possibly in both your professional and personal life.

Tactic: Stop, look both ways, and proceed with a better understanding of what's ahead.

For leaders this means ensuring that we take the time to pause before and throughout the execution of organizational change. This is to ensure an understanding of the organization's landscape as well as what is in the employee's control and what is not. It means using the word *mandatory* if applicable and describing the *why* behind our actions.

Leaders should err on the side of over-communication and follow-up. Rounding with targeted questions related to the organizational change serves as a great way to check in with employees on an individual level. Employee forums can also be enhanced by including relevant updates on the external environment. Remember, adult learners need multiple platforms in how information is distributed, so mix it up with verbal and written communication formats.

Roadblock #2: The Unexpected Detour

Unexpected detours occur most commonly when changes are made in work flow and processes. They're a kind of roadblock that can be managed through focus, time, or other resources. The individual employee might be able to make some degree of progress in overcoming this particular inhibitor to performance; however, most detours are handled more effectively when managed by leadership and approached as a team effort.

An example of a common unexpected detour that's best managed by leaders is a change in funding for a specific project or department, requiring employees to do more with less. (Perhaps an unexpected crisis, such as snow, a hurricane, or a tornado, has diverted funding and rearranged organizational priorities.) The goal and expected outcome for the work has not changed, just the resources available to get it done. It may take months before a leader can get back to the original goals set prior to the crisis, and even longer for the budget to return to normal.

Remember, just as annoying detours along the roads we travel make us crazy, unexpected organizational detours can make employees feel stressed, annoyed, and exasperated. We *all* eventually adjust to detours both at work and on the road, but it often takes us a minute to wrap our heads around the new changes required.

Tactic: Prompt your GPS to "recalculate."

Leaders *are* the organization's GPS. They set direction (strategic goals), choose the best route (action plans), and along the way often have to recalculate their approach in order to manage roadblocks or get to the goal destination faster. To facilitate success for those responsible for execution, leaders must be the voice that guides employees turn by turn. To do this, identify the goal, the plan, and anticipated detours early on, and then create a communication plan for all employees affected.

Think back over your own leadership tenure. When was the last time you shared your action plan(s) and progress to date with your employees? Do they know about the detours and new directions that you need to implement? Remember, they may need a minute or two to wrap their heads around the changes. Early knowledge and inclusion in the recalculating process helps get employees to the desired results faster.

Roadblock #3: The Backseat Driver

We hear them whispering in our ears, "Why are you going this way? We have always gone the other direction. Why change now?" Or perhaps we hear, "Great job! I like this new route to…"

These are backseat drivers. They have their own beliefs and perceptions about performance and how we should spend our time. Backseat drivers can be other leaders, employees, consumers, and even community members. Just one vocal person can impact the successful execution of organizational change—for better or worse.

Within your team, you'll probably find that higher performers are often open to change and are willing to figure out the best way to approach the new roadblock. (In other words, they help you navigate.) Average performers may be stymied by the roadblock—not sure whether to turn back or proceed with caution. (In other words, they're simply along for the ride and don't have much to contribute.) It's the lower performers who will often create a long list of (usually unfounded) reasons why the roadblock is preventing them from getting things done, and why your organization or department should *not* change. (These are your backseat drivers!)

Tactic: Listen and communicate. (Don't just turn up the radio to drown out your backseat drivers!)

Even though backseat drivers may distract you, the leader, from your journey, it is your job to listen to them and manage the exchange. Here's an exercise you can use to facilitate dialogue, clarify misinformation, and define the game plan when you find yourself riding with a backseat driver.

- Instruct a group of employees to list all the roadblocks to accomplishing the desired organizational change on a flip chart. (This exercise works best with groups of 20 or less.) Ask them to be specific and to explain the *why* behind their answers.

- Then have the group identify which type of roadblock they believe they're up against: The Stop Sign (something out of their control), The Unexpected Detour (unanticipated changes to work flow and processes), or The Backseat Driver (based on perceptions or beliefs).

- Focus on the second two roadblocks and determine what employees need in order to move beyond these roadblocks for success. This is a great table exercise. If the list is long, have your employees pick the top three roadblocks they would like to work on. If acceptable, incorporate these into relevant 90-day action plans and be sure to follow up with results to date.

- Leaders need to own the first type of roadblock and create a plan about how to improve communication regarding the rollout of Stop Sign messages.

- Leaders must directly address the persistent voices of low performers. Be clear about acceptable and unacceptable behavior.

Roadblocks do not have to get in the way of achieving organizational results or consume valuable time in the face of change. If they are identified early and handled efficiently through a thoughtful plan of action, improved results will invariably follow.

Job Bundling

Leaders have the difficult job of handling many different types of duties, so combining similar tasks allows you to switch gears fewer times throughout the day. This process makes you more efficient in accomplishing your multiple tasks.

Job bundling requires pre-planning and working with your support staff to ensure that schedules are set up in a way that minimizes the number of mental switches you are required to do in a workday. For instance, if you have monthly meetings with your direct reports, why not group them in one or two targeted days? This allows you to stay focused on similar topics and approaches. The same goes for travel outside of your home office. Think about grouping appointments by proximity so you don't waste time driving all over town.

In addition, we all have times of the day when we're better at handling different types of tasks. If you're a morning person, you probably zip through technical tasks between the hours of

8:00 a.m. and 11:00 a.m. You likely hit your mid-afternoon slump around 2:00 p.m. and prefer to focus on more creative, "lighter" pursuits then. Bundling your tasks allows you to take advantage of your own work rhythm.

Manage Your Meetings

There is nothing more frustrating than leaving a meeting with your boss feeling as if nothing was accomplished and that it was a total waste of time! Or maybe the meeting got completely derailed by a topic you were not prepared to discuss. When you aren't the leader of the meeting you may feel that there is little you can do to change things (hence, the frustration I mentioned).

However, if you *are* the boss, there is plenty you can do.

So ask yourself: *What can I do to have more meaningful meetings that facilitate moving my organization's results and building better relationships with my direct reports?* Here are some tips to consider:

- **Make sure both parties come prepared.**
    - ° The supervisor should review current organizational results that the employee is accountable for and action plans that impact them *before* the meeting. Be sure to highlight priorities. In addition, identify any additional topics for the meeting and send to direct reports in advance (one week). This offers the employee the opportunity to review their own performance to date before the meeting and come prepared.

○ Direct reports should review their current results and action plans before the meeting and send their highest priorities to their supervisor. They should be prepared to discuss any additional areas of focus previously identified.

- **Use an agenda template for consistency in approach and to maintain focus.**

  Studer Group has designed and implemented a standardized agenda for monthly meetings between leaders that may be a useful platform to help you increase effectiveness and efficiency. The recommended meeting time is 60 minutes each month and contains the following key elements:

  ○ **Relationship Building.** Start the meeting with five minutes of discussion that focuses more on the "personal" elements of the relationship. "How was your son's graduation?" "Are you and the family all ready for your cruise next month?" These kinds of questions let the employee relate to you on a more human level. What they hear is *I care about you as a person and what's important to you.* Starting the meeting this way sets the tone for a more positive and open discussion about performance.

  ○ **Review of Performance.** Remember, the role of any leader is to move organizational results, so the majority of the meeting should focus on current performance to date as it relates to achieving targeted results. Use an 80/20 rule, with 80 percent of the meeting focused on review of performance and the rest of the meeting on all other business. This should include:

- Recognition of positive trends and out-comes.

- Addressing barriers to achieving desired outcomes.

- Validation (observation/documentation) of the actions being taken to address gaps in performance.

- Agree on next steps.

- Identifying communication strategy, if needed. (Inadequate communication or miscommunication is a major time robber. Be proactive in reducing these occurrences.)

Recommendation: Start with a review of the direct report's results (i.e., balanced scorecards, financial outcomes, project status) then move to the action plans. Discuss alignment between the current results and projected plans to change them. Are assigned actions realistic, including the time needed to execute successfully? Are there opportunities to collaborate with other employees or departments to increase efficiency and effectiveness (thus saving more time and limiting rework)?

○ **Review of Current Staffing or Operational Challenges Not Covered in Review of Results.** Beware, this is an area that can derail an entire meeting, especially if you and the direct report are talking about a difficult employee. Try and limit the discussion to one or two items that carry the highest priority or urgency. The direct report should be prepared to outline the issue, confirm actions taken to date, and communicate what they need from their supervisor. Again, preparation is the key to maximizing meeting effectiveness. If an entire meeting is needed to discuss an employee concern, schedule a separate meeting allowing complete focus on that subject.

○ **Include a Periodic Check-in on Professional Development.** At least quarterly, there should be a discussion on how the employee is moving forward in their professional growth and development. This could include conference attendance, skill development, and annual assessments on key competencies. This offers you, the leader, an opportunity to clarify expectations throughout the year instead of just during the time of the annual performance evaluation. Clarity of expectations creates a more effective work environment. (Another time robber is time wasted wondering what your boss wants you to do!)

○ **Confirm Action Items for Follow-up and Document Items to Address During Next Meeting.** Once you get into this rhythm, the meetings become focused. Each party knows what will be discussed and comes fully prepared. If something arises before the next meeting, forcing a change in the agenda (as it often will), make sure you and the other person are in mutual agreement regarding the revised areas of focus. This ensures adequate preparation.

° **Cancel and Reschedule the Meeting If Parties Are Not Prepared.** Don't waste each other's precious time.

° **Additional Tips.** Each participant in the meeting should review materials that will be covered in advance. Either party requiring a decision should send information in advance. This way, no surprises are introduced during the meeting. Use impact messages when there are gaps in performance rather than making excuses.

Just Let Go and Delegate!

Leaders need to understand when to let someone else take on a task—and how to let that person make it her own. Learning to delegate is a skill that will help you find balance in your abundant workload. It's so easy, as a leader, to want to accomplish everything yourself. However, getting caught up in small day-to-day tasks takes a toll on your overall efficiency and stops you from seeing the big picture.

Delegation is not just handing off your responsibilities to someone else to save time. It actually is a much more thoughtful process that maximizes the potential of your workforce, impacts outcomes, and enhances teamwork. And successful teamwork always enhances efficiency. Here are some of the benefits of delegation:

• **Workforce Development.** When you delegate, you will help your employees learn new skills and give them the opportunity to develop themselves and achieve their goals. This makes them more versatile and a more important part of your team. It also shows that you have trust and confidence in them.

- **Increased Flexibility.** Have you ever been in a situation where a key employee needed for a job is on vacation or out sick? When you delegate tasks to your employees, try to move the tasks around to different employees. This will increase the skills of everyone and the flexibility of your team. Plus, you'll have an alternative when one employee is unavailable and unable to fulfill the needed task. This is the premise behind cross-training in organizations.

- **Balanced Workloads.** When you delegate effectively, you can make sure that everyone has an equal amount of work. The perceived fairness in spreading out the work will gain you respect from your team members. This can also enhance your credibility as a leader.

- **Better Solutions to Problems.** Sometimes leaders get trapped in their own heads, thinking they are the only ones with the best way to approach a problem or task. Delegation allows others who may have valuable ideas to offer more effective and efficient approaches. At a minimum, it will open up a dialogue that enhances clarity in purpose and in necessary actions.

Clear the Mud

Have you ever looked in a pool of murky water and wondered what treasures might be hiding below the surface? Our imagination takes us in so many different directions that it is highly unlikely that two or more people would ever imagine the same thing. We could envision beautiful fish with an array of colors or a stinky old boot. We won't really know what is hiding there until the mud settles and the water clears. Only then do we find the real answer.

This is a great analogy for how we as leaders often communicate. Our unfocused or vague communications are like a pool of murky water. Sometimes our colleagues and staff are left wondering about the true meaning of our messages (what lies below) and we—without meaning to!—leave it up to their imaginations to fill in the blanks. The result is often confusion, frustration (sender and receiver), and misalignment.

This lack of clarity or specificity in communication can be a major barrier to successfully executing actions that achieve organizational results and impact critical relationships in the workplace. And it goes without saying that being as clear as possible greatly impacts those valuable leadership minutes!

Here's a typical scenario to consider…

How often have we said, "I'll have that report to you by the end of the day"?

Is this an example of clear communication or is it mud? When *is* the end of the day? Is it the end of the day for me personally, for my department, for my location? Is it Eastern Standard Time or Central Time? For some people, the end of the day is when they go to bed at night. "End of the day" is just not a specific enough time to have meaning. It would be much better to say, "I will have this on your desk by next Friday, September 7, at 3:00 p.m. Central." This denotes a specific day and time that is in no way ambiguous.

Because this commitment is so concise and clear, it is difficult to misinterpret. As specificity goes up, miscommunication goes down. But something else also occurs. Clarity enhances accountability and cuts down on wasted time trying to figure out the true meanings behind our words! As a leader, you must include specific deadlines and timelines in your communication. These simple additional words increase productivity and decrease stress levels and confusion.

REMEMBER:

A deadline is when work is due.

A timeline is when work gets done.

**And when work gets done,
strategic results are achieved!**

Here are some tips to help "clear the mud" and add clarity to your communication:

- **Do your homework!** Ask yourself the following questions:
    - ° What are the essential messages I want to communicate?
    - ° Are the messages tailored for the target audience?
    - ° Have I "connected to purpose" or explained the *why* in terms that the target audience can relate to?

- ° Have I included key stakeholders prior to communicating the message to a larger audience?

- ° Am I trying to communicate too many messages at the same time? (Remember, most people can digest and retain only one or two items at a time. You may want to consider breaking up the message as appropriate.)

- ° Have I achieved the right tone for the message? Beware of the natural tendency to start bad news with celebration to soften the blow. Most people appreciate and respect a more direct approach. Spend more time connecting the *why* for the bad news than worrying over how you will cushion it.

- ° Have I described and provided a visual of the behaviors and deadlines required for good job performance?

- ° Can my request be measured?

- ° Is it realistic for this person or team to achieve and accomplish my request within the stated timelines?

- ° Does this request move us closer to our objective?

- ° What milestones will ensure that we are on the right track to accomplish our goals?

- ° Do I need to communicate this message multiple times in a variety of forums?

- **Rehearse the delivery if possible.** For complex or sensitive messages, you may want to verbalize the message and the approach with another leader. Feedback from others can give you the opportunity to course correct prior to delivery. Sometimes when we act in isolation, we are unable to hear how our own words may land on others. This approach can also work with written communication. Have other eyes read your message before you send.

- **Know when to use e-mail and when to use the spoken word.** Do a self-audit. Are you overusing e-mail to communicate important information or to avoid a situation that may be uncomfortable on the phone or in person? Choose your vehicle for communicating wisely. Quick e-mails may be easy, but they may not yield the desired results. Nothing major, like big changes or sensitive issues, should be communicated in e-mail.

  If you do choose to use e-mail, read your message twice before you hit the send button. Finally, never e-mail anyone in anger. You may find it difficult to pull back the message and its impact once it has been sent.

- **Be prepared for one-on-one meetings with employees.** A little review never hurt anyone! As I recommended earlier in this chapter, always have a pre-determined agenda for discussion. Remember, any materials that can be sent ahead of the meeting for review increase its effectiveness. If time is limited, keep your meetings focused with an objective in mind. Check in with your partner at the beginning of the meeting to ensure that your objectives align. And before the close of the meeting, make sure both parties agree to next steps, who's accountable for what, and timeframes for completion of identified tasks. Follow up with an e-mail summarizing key takeaways.

- **Keep messaging consistent across the leadership team.**

- ° Do you have a unified approach to how key messages are communicated to employees? This is an important step for success.

- ° Are agendas for staff meetings standardized by strategic priorities (i.e., Finance, Growth, Customer Service, Workplace of Choice, Quality)? The discussion items may vary from leader to leader under each priority area, but the entire organization should stay focused on the goals they are trying to achieve. This entails constantly "connecting the dots" for employees and their work.

- **Align your verbal and non-verbal messages.** Do the words you speak match your face or body language? For example, when the words you use say, "I am listening" but your eyes are on your computer, the message is, "I am not listening." How many times have you heard, "I have an open door policy"; however, when you enter the room, the leader never stops what they are doing to really hear you? They might not even face you or make eye contact. Their body language screams, "I am busy, so get it over with quickly." Enough said.

- **Follow up on critical communication.** Even if you cannot deliver on a specific request, respond anyway with the *why*. Others appreciate hearing (and often deserve to hear!) the reason you cannot move forward.

As leaders, no matter what role we hold in an organization, we must be master communicators. Ninety percent or more of our day is spent transmitting messages, receiving messages, analyzing messages, and designing messages. Sometimes we even wish some messages would disappear!

The right message can motivate thousands to follow you or change behaviors. A wrong or poorly constructed message can fuel negativity, disconnect others from the goals you are trying to achieve, and consume valuable leadership minutes! Leaders must spend the mental energy it takes to ensure that we are communicating as effectively as possible and maximizing all the tools available to us. Sometimes, we have only one shot to deliver the "right message" to the "right audience" to achieve the desired result.

Communicating with Difficult Employees

Meet Tom. He is one of your colleagues (peer leader) whose behavior regularly interferes with your ability to get along with him—and on many occasions his actions affect your ability to get your work done effectively and *on time*.

Tom seems completely unmanageable and seems to take perverse pleasure in not getting along with those around him. You have tried talking to him, but nothing seems to be working. The office rumor mill has labeled him a difficult person.

You have mentally put Tom into a passive/aggressive box. You are frustrated and want to have a better working relationship but don't know where to begin.

Sound familiar? I am sure we all have had a Tom cross our path during our career journey. And if you haven't yet, you most likely will, so watch out!

Keep the following points in mind when dealing with someone you consider difficult:

- Something you say or do could trigger the behavior that annoys you the most.

- Chances are the other person doesn't realize that you are upset with them.

- Difficult people may provoke you in different ways: demanding attention by overwhelming others, holding back anger and keeping it to themselves, talking endlessly about what (to you) seems like irrelevant trivia, rarely smiling or being pleasant, or manipulating everyone.

- Sometimes the organizational culture or limited resources can bring out the worst in all of us.

- Remember, the perception of "difficult" is through your lens or the lens of others and may not be a universally shared perception of the employee in question.

- The heart of effective communication is relationships.

Here are some tips to consider when trying to improve the way you communicate with a difficult person. If this is a direct report and the behavior crosses into a disciplinary issue, these tips can be very helpful as a first approach to address the problem. You may need to initiate a more formal process if the behavior continues.

- Look to yourself first. Communication always goes in two directions. Are you doing anything to provoke the behaviors that annoy you the most? Are you overreacting to what the other person is doing?

- Separate the behavior from the person. Recognize that the difficulty is in the relationship, not necessarily the person. It's a matter of how you perceive each other. Do you have different perspectives, different values, different cultures, or different life experiences? To communicate in spite of these differences, listen, check your own behavior and reactions, have direct and respectful discussions with the perceived "difficult person," and remain open to resolution.

- Look for special circumstances that produce special behaviors (e.g., sick child, financial issues, school, etc.). Are you managing your reactions to transient or uncommon behaviors? If the variables influencing behavior are within your control, are there ways to improve these dynamics?

- Openly and calmly discuss the challenge in the relationship. Respectful truth telling can begin to form the basis of genuine change. Beware of letting emotion take over the discussion.

- Be willing to accept each other for who you are. Listen and look for areas of compromise or negotiation. Ask for support in creating a positive change in the relationship.

- Be an active participant. Things never just "take care of themselves."

Key Phrases: Communicating with Someone Who Knows It All

- "That's an interesting perspective."
- "What do you think of...?"

- "When you talk like that, I get upset because..."
- "I'd like you to consider these alternatives."

Key Phrases: Breaking the Silence Barrier

- "I really do want to know what you are thinking/feeling."
- "We need your contribution in order to..."
- "Your participation is important to us."

Communicating with difficult people is never easy. Difficult people often don't pay much attention to their own behavior or realize how others feel about them. But we must still deal with these individuals.

When you are in a leadership position, everyone looks to you to steer the team toward success. Even though it can be daunting to be in charge, know that everyone respects a leader who is calm, efficient, and excited to pursue excellence. In fact, many employees will emulate such leaders. There are so many things you can do to maximize the minutes you have each day. Choose one or two tactics to focus on as you begin to take firmer charge of your time. As you learn to align your own priorities, you will become a stronger leader and may even inspire your employees to take control of their professional and personal lives, too.

"If you want to do a few small things right, do them yourself. If you want to do great things and make a big impact, learn to delegate."

— John C. Maxwell

The Struggle Is Real!

"Seventy-five percent of my life is spent wasting time. The other 25 percent isn't nearly as productive."

—Jarod Kintz

Wait a Hot Minute! was created to offer you a resource on how to manage your life in the minutes you have each day…1,440 daily…525,600 valuable minutes each year. This is never an easy task or one that can be solved by just focusing on managing the use of technology or taking scheduled breaks throughout the day. It takes a true self-assessment of how you use all your minutes to improve and add value to the quality of your life—mind, body, and spirit.

Each day we are given the opportunity to choose our path. Yes, there is still the reality of work and family priorities that may consume many of our daily minutes. However, we also make other choices described throughout the book that deduct minutes from our life and offer us nothing in return.

Some of these choices are sheer habits that are hard to break, like using our smartphones as if we would wither without a peek at those screens several times an hour (and sometimes more than that!). Other choices fulfill obligations imposed by others and prohibit us from taking the time needed to take care of ourselves. And some choices occur because we have not hit the pause button long enough to determine what we are missing, what we need, and how we could better use the minutes we have each day.

There is no magic potion you can take to become a better you. The only person controlling your "hot minutes" is YOU! The struggle to manage time in our lives is real. We may not be able to completely eliminate all our wasted minutes, but minimizing the waste is very doable. It's amazing how we can find the will to do almost anything if it is something we value. The question I have for you is: What do you value enough to reset your daily clock?

Use *Wait a Hot Minute!* to pick out a few problem areas or wasted minutes that resonate with you and begin. Write down the changes you want to make and share these commitments with a partner for additional support. There is a commitment log in the book to help you, but feel free to use your own paper or even start a journal if you wish.

Start small and increase your efforts from there. Reclaiming even 10 minutes a day is a great start that will result in a new you. You will find that once you start resetting your daily clock, you will want to do even more.

Every day I wake up thinking about what I have to do from sunup until I am back in the warmth of my bed again. Some days I am successful at carving out time just for me. This is usually in the quiet of early morning, when no one else is awake and I can just "be." Other days, I struggle with conflicting priorities and get overwhelmed with minute-stealing demands.

I am determined to reset my clock one minute at a time. I know I won't be perfect, but for me and those I love, it is imperative that I try. I now limit my use of technology (smartphones, Internet, etc.) after 7:00 p.m. each night so that I can spend quality time with my family and actually *hear* what they are saying. My anxiety level rises (for no good reason) when I hear the beep of the phone signaling a new message, and I force myself not to pick it up in that minute to respond— trying to honor my commitment to myself about the use of my time. I schedule (like an appointment) exercise each week. Now, I may not make it to the class or gym, but that's a choice as well—to stay home and catch up on some much-needed sleep. Oh yes, the struggle is real.

We are always so quick to say, "I don't have time," but the truth is we really do have time and we have choices in how to spend it. When you put "hot minutes" in perspective, 10 minutes out of 1,440 daily minutes *is* doable. That means you have 1,430 minutes left to waste, if you like. Think about it.

"Your hand can seize today, but not tomorrow; and thoughts of your tomorrow are nothing but desire. Don't waste this breath, if your heart isn't crazy, since 'the rest of your life' won't last forever."

—Omar Khayyám

Key Hot Minutes: Quick Chapter Reference

For those readers who would like to feature this book at book clubs or various discussion groups, this section provides you with key messages found in each chapter to help focus the dialogue.

Introduction: How Did We Arrive in This Place?

It's really not the multitasking that's "bad"—after all, a certain amount of it is inevitable—but the frantic tangle of trying to get everything done at once is not the best way to live (and enjoy) our lives. We've been struggling to better manage our minutes since the dawn of time, and all these years later, not much has changed. Though we have all the conveniences of modern life, the minutes making up our days have stayed the same over the years: 1,440 hot minutes with which to order our lives in an efficient and well-organized manner.

Chapter 1: The Time Machine

Shifts in the way people work and live have changed the way leisure time is experienced and who gets to experience it. Years ago, low-paid blue-collar workers were more likely to punch in a long day than their professional counterparts. Today, professionals are working long hours too. And there are blurred lines between work and play. There's no work off-switch and there's less time for play.

Most of us do not want to make the sacrifices needed to live comfortably within 24 hours. Nor do we wish to make tough choices that would decrease stress and anxiety in our lives. The personal and professional commitment to improving the quality of your life and maximizing your time is totally in your hands. It is a never-ending discipline with an incredible end result that benefits not only you but others around you.

Effectively managing your 24-hour timeframe can sharpen your focus and the precision of the tasks of the day. Pacing your tasks may dramatically reduce the amount of rework when you are well rested and focused.

Even though the number of hours has not changed, our perception of "a day" can vary for a workday, weekend day, vacation day, sick day, or holiday. Each perception is influenced by the value and importance of the day or expectations of others.

Getting a good night's sleep must move up on your priority list. Self-assess how different levels of sleep affect you. You should aim for the number of hours you need for peak performance (mentally and physically).

Important factors for being able to adjust to an extended workday more than likely relate to characteristics such as age, marital status, parental status, hobbies, and personal interests.

On the surface, technology like iPhones appears to be a great time saver, but it can cause you to use up more of your time trying to fix miscommunication inherent in just using written words or the cryptic language of texting. A real human-to-human connection adds tone and texture to the discussion. Face time gives you non-verbal cues that help tell a complete story. There is also a higher probability that you will maintain a single focus in a face-to-face discussion and not get drawn into the multitasking cycle.

Societal evolution and new variables like advances in technology (good or bad) have created generational differences in how we interact with the world. Younger workers (25-44 years of age) are more likely to be employed part-time in an attempt to improve their quality of life (defined by the workers as more downtime). Older workers (45 years of age and above) work full-time to improve their quality of life (defined by the workers as financial stability). Our perception of time and how we choose to prioritize its use seems to be directly related to what we value. Multiple researchers proclaim that what we value is age related.

Key tips for mothers to consider in trying to maximize their minutes:

- Minimize distractions and the tendency to multitask. In other words, focus on each daily task.

- Set reasonable daily goals—we *are not* superheroes.

- Don't seek perfectionism.

We all need time to play, in order to mentally and physically recharge. Play adds joy to life, relieves stress, supercharges learning, and connects you to others and the world around you.

Chapter 2: Time Robbers: Stealing Our Lives One "Hot Minute" at a Time

Time robbers are the people or the things that distract us from achieving what we set out to do. In the long run, we lose pieces of ourselves along the way. The most common time robbers include:

The "big four":

- Poor listening

- Becoming sheep

- Moving papers

- Misaligned or changing priorities

Other time robbers include:

- Electronics

- Constant crises at home and work

- Meetings without purpose

- Disorganization

- Poor communication

- Unclear responsibility and authority

- Procrastination/indecision

- Ineffective delegation

- Inability to say no

- Multitasking

Chapter 3: Maximizing Your Minutes: Tips for Effective Time Management

After true "time robbers" are identified from your personal analysis, pick one or two that are the most wasteful. Then look for a few simple remedies to reduce the "time robbers." Remedies may include: planning your day by listing what must get done, controlling interruptions, setting aside stated office hours, and shortening your meetings. Do not rely upon others to determine your time priorities. You are the only person who is qualified to judge the importance of all the things you must do in a given day.

Since breathing is something you can control, it is a useful tool for achieving a relaxed and clear state of mind. There are many practitioners that teach a variety of breathing techniques world-wide. Many are grounded in the arts of meditation, tai chi, and yoga. The commonality across all these techniques is the ability of the participant to focus and let go—one minute at a time. You may want to try several techniques to see which one works for you.

The Internet is an essential tool for most people today but there are still those who do not realize that they are wasting time by using it. Managing your Internet usage helps you become more effective in your life and can also improve your productivity as a whole. With Internet time management in place, you can refocus on the important aspects of life.

We are a conflict avoidance culture. We will dodge having to say no by any means necessary. But sometimes, saying no is the most respectful thing you can do for the requester. It actually can save you both time. You get out of something that you didn't want to do. The requester moves on to someone who really wants to participate.

Saying no in the workplace can be anxiety provoking, as employers today expect us to do more in less time. When someone makes a request at work, think before you respond. Hit the pause button and allow yourself time to evaluate the cost/benefit of saying yes. If you still come to the conclusion that no is the best answer, respond in a timely way and ask if there is another way you can contribute. In other words, offer an alternative to no. This lets the employer know you understand your limits, but care about the task at hand and the company (a great characteristic for a leader).

Not everything we do offers an immediate time-saving benefit. Some actions, like collaboration with others on your team, are an investment for future savings. This truth could apply to your circle of family, friends, or coworkers. A side benefit of collaboration is the mutual ownership of the results achieved when your team is engaged.

Here's the short tip for gaining back your minutes: STOP OWNING OTHER FOLKS' STUFF! Hold those around you—even your children—accountable for their responsibilities. They need to value their minutes and respect yours! Don't let "never mind" be the rule, but rather the exception. Don't be fooled into thinking owning other folks' stuff will get you more time. It actually sucks the life out of you on so many levels.

It doesn't take much to move toward a more purposeful life. Start by adding a few things that "fill your cup" and bring you joy. And begin eliminating things that are just time consuming with very little or no return. Those activities usually drain your energy for things that are (or should be) a higher priority.

Chapter 4: What Can You Do In…? (Small Blocks of Hot Minutes Really Add Up!)

Success in managing your life in minutes starts by developing achievable goals for each day. Decide which goals you want to achieve. Estimate how long it will take you in minutes, being sure to leave some minutes for the unexpected. Schedule your day so that your number-one goal receives the majority of your time. Don't procrastinate by tackling the unimportant tasks or tasks that could be accomplished on another day.

Chapter 5: But, I'm the Boss! How to Take Charge of Your Time When You're in Charge of EVERYTHING

For those in leadership roles, more time is taken struggling with "how we do things." This makes us lose focus on the most important priorities that drive results. **Eighty percent of your results come from 20 percent of your activities!** It's your responsibility to yourself and your team to know where your highest payoff activities are and eliminate as many as you can of the ones that yield few results.

Most leaders have three primary areas where they can make changes that will lead to major time improvement: prioritizing/organizing, interruptions, and meetings.

Leaders with strong time management and organizational skills are able to demonstrate powerful techniques for their team members, making everyone more productive. Key factors in strong time management are: being aware of the vision, setting specific and realistic goals, setting and communicating priorities, and having the discipline to follow the plan.

High Impact Tools in 10 Minutes or Less

Rounding can be one of the most powerful tools in your leadership toolbox. It allows leaders to proactively engage, listen, communicate, build relationships, and support our most important customers—our employees.

Huddles are a powerful team builder and accelerator for consistency in execution. In just 5-10 minutes, the leader can brief the staff on unit/departmental goals, progress to date, connect to purpose, and reward and recognize accomplishments. The end result is a team that is reenergized, focused, and ready to go.

An old-fashioned handwritten thank-you note can go a long way to build relationships with coworkers.

"Note to Self: I don't have to take this day all at once, but rather one step, one breath, one moment at a time. I am only one person. Things will get done when they get done."

—Anonymous Author

I Want My Minutes!

Here's My Personal Commitment

Today, I affirm I will value how I use all the minutes I have in 24 hours.

These are the top three things I will start doing today (include how many hot minutes each step will impact):

Task/Action	Hot Minutes Impacted

These are the top three things I will stop doing today (include how many hot minutes each step will impact):

Task/Action	Hot Minutes Impacted

Here are the things I need help with:

My supporters, personally and professionally (these are the people with whom you will share this affirmation and ask to be your mirror to stay on track):

Name:

Date of Commitment:

Acknowledgments

Writing this book has truly been a labor of love and discovery over the last year. As with most things we accomplish in life, many people contribute to our success. This has certainly been the case in completing this book. Whether it was sharing their stories, friendly edits, being my sounding board, or just holding my hand, each person played a significant role in this body of work that I am honored to share with you. I will be forever grateful for their gifts to me.

Although you always take the risk of leaving someone out, there are a few people I would like to offer a special thank-you:

Wesley Gaines, my husband of 40 years, has held my hand through all my personal struggles with time. Any decisions I have made regarding how I use my valuable minutes each day directly impact the quality of our life. They have not always been the right decisions, but we have always worked through them together. Some of my lessons learned along the way have been influenced by his never-ending wisdom.

To my children and grandchildren for putting up with me as I have attempted to work through the time challenges of being a working mom/grandma. The added variable of being a leader in healthcare for most of my career often made managing my minutes impossible. However, my children and grandchildren serve as constant reminders of what is really important and why I must take the time to *wait a hot minute*!

To two courageous women, Anna Anthony Valle and Kim Titcomb Saguinsin, who agreed to share their personal stories. Their challenges and wins in the daily battle with time offer hope to those who seem to be lost in the craziness of their lives. I am sure you will find a little piece of yourself in their truths and be motivated to rethink how you use your hot minutes.

To all my family and friends for lending their voices to the numerous surveys I conducted in social media about the value of time and what makes a difference. Factual accounts can offer one side of the story. Listening to the voices of our diverse culture adds texture to the existing research on this subject.

To Quint Studer and B.G. Porter, I will forever be grateful for your leadership. Thank you for bringing me into Studer Group and believing in me.

To Bekki Kennedy, a Fire Starter in every way, thank you for your guidance. Your passion and dedication to publishing resources that make a positive difference have made a lasting impact on healthcare.

To Lindy Sikes and Jamie Stewart for your help, attention to every detail, and getting this book into the hands of those who will benefit from it.

To Dottie DeHart & Company for your thoughtful assistance in moving this book from manuscript to finished product.

I am so grateful for contributions large and small. They each have added to the depth of this book, which is hopefully a wonderful tool for you to maximize your hot minutes.

Fondly,

Jackie

References

Introduction:

1. Sullivan, Meg. "Think Multitasking is New? Our Prehistoric Ancestors Invented It, UCLA Book Argues," *UCLA Newsroom*, December 7, 2010. http://newsroom.ucla.edu/releases/new-ucla-book-traces-suprisingly-179731

Chapter 1:

1. Seneca, Lucius Annaeus. *On the Shortness of Life: Penguin Great Ideas edition.* Edited and Translated by C.D.N. Costa. London: Penguin, 2005. Pg. 45.

2. Canadian Centre for Occupational Health and Safety. "Fatigue Fact Sheet." Last modified February 17, 2012. https://www.ccohs.ca/oshanswers/psychosocial/fatigue.html

3. Evans, Lisa. "The Exact Amount of Time You Should Work Every Day," *Fast Company*, September 15, 2014.

http://www.fastcompany.com/3035605/how-to-be-a-success-at-everything/the-exact-amount-of-time-you-should-work-every-day

4. Greenfield, David. *Virtual Addiction: Sometimes New Technology Can Create New Problems* (blog) http://drdavidgreenfield.com/virtual-addiction/

5. The Nielsen Company. "The Total Audience Report 2015," New York: CZT/CAN Trademarks. December 10, 2015. http://www.nielsen.com/us/en/insights/reports/2015/the-total-audience-report-q3-2015.html

6. Young, Kimberly, and Cristiano Nabuco de Abreu. *Internet Addiction: A Handbook and Guide to Evaluation and Treatment.* Hoboken: John Wiley & Sons, 2010. Pg. 225.

7. Center for Internet and Technology Addiction. "Virtual Addiction Test," http://virtual-addiction.com/virtual-addiction-test/

8. De Meuse, Kenneth P., Thomas J. Bergmann, and Scott W. Lester. "An Investigation of the Relational Component of the Psychological Contract across Time, Generation, and Employment Status," *Journal of Managerial Issues* 13 (2001): 102-118. http://www.jstor.org/stable/40604336.

9. Patota, Nancy, Deborah Schwartz, and Theodore Schwartz. "Leveraging Generational Differences for Productivity Gains," *The Journal of American Academy of Business, Cambridge* 11 (2007). Pg. 3.

10. Workfront, Inc. "The Work-Life Imbalance Report," April 2015. https://www.workfront.com/enterprise/resource/ebook/work-life-imbalance/

11. Parker, Kim, and Wendy Wang. "Modern Parenthood: Roles of Moms and Dads Converge as They Balance Work and Family," Washington, DC: Pew Research Center. March 14, 2013. http://www.pewsocialtrends.org/2013/03/14/modern-parenthood-roles-of-moms-and-dads-converge-as-they-balance-work-and-family/

12. LaRowe, Michelle. *Working Mom's 411: How to Manage Kids, Career, and Home.* Ventura: Regal, 2009.

Chapter 3:

1. Merriam-Webster Online, s.v. "importance," accessed February 19, 2016, http://www.merriam-webster.com/dictionary/importance.

2. Ibid, http://www.merriam-webster.com/dictionary/urgency.

3. Harvard Health Publications, "Relaxation Techniques: Breath Control Health Quell Errant Stress Response." January 26, 2015. http://www.health.harvard.edu/mind-and-mood/relaxation-techniques-breath-control-helps-quell-errant-stress-response

4. Hansen, Drew. "A Guide to Mindfulness at Work," *Forbes*, October 31, 2012, http://www.forbes.com/sites/drewhansen/2012/10/31/a-guide-to-mindfulness-at-work/#f2f49306870d

5. Ibid.

6. Kelly, Caitlin. "O.K., Google, Take a Deep Breath." *The New York Times*, April 28, 2012. http://www.nytimes.com/2012/04/29/technology/google-course-asks-employees-to-take-a-deep-breath.html

7. Steiner-Adair, Catherine, and Teresa H. Barker. *The Big Disconnect: Protecting Childhood and Family Relationships in the Digital Age.* New York: HarperCollins, 2013.

8. Hinnant, Amanda. "10 Guilt-Free Strategies for Saying No," *Real Simple,* http://www.realsimple.com/work-life/10-guilt-free-strategies-for-saying-no

9. Lawton, Ian. "10 Ways to Know You are Taking Too Much Responsibility," *Soul Seeds* (blog). http://www.soul-seeds.com/grapevine/2011/10/how-to-know-you-are-taking-too-much-responsibility/

Chapter 5:

1. Wainwright, Corey. "You're Going to Waste 31 Hours in Meetings This Month," *HubSpot Marketing* (blog). http://blog.hubspot.com/marketing/time-wasted-meetings-data#sm.0000hsykntkw7fius8v1us1pfxsjz

2. Studer, Quint. *Hardwiring Excellence: Purpose, Worthwhile Work, Making a Difference.* Gulf Breeze: Fire Starter, 2003. Pg. 143.

3. Shipley, Erin. "Using Shift Huddles to Empower Leaders," *Insights Blog.* https://www.studergroup.com/resources/news-media/healthcare-publications-resources/insights/april-2016/using-shift-huddles-to-empower-leaders

Additional Resources

ABOUT STUDER GROUP®, A HURON HEALTH-CARE SOLUTION:

Learn more about Studer Group® by scanning the QR code with your mobile device or by visiting www.studergroup.com/who-we-are/about-studer-group.

A recipient of the 2010 Malcolm Baldrige National Quality Award, Studer Group is an outcomes-based healthcare performance improvement firm that works with healthcare organizations in the United States, Canada, and beyond, teaching them how to achieve, sustain, and accelerate exceptional clinical, operational, and financial results. Working together, we help to get the foundation right so organizations can build a sustainable culture that promotes accountability, fosters innovation, and consistently delivers a great patient experience and the best quality outcomes over time.

To learn more about Studer Group, a Huron Healthcare solution, visit www.studergroup.com or call 850-439-5839.

STUDER GROUP COACHING:

Learn more about Studer Group coaching by scanning the QR code with your mobile device or by visiting www.studergroup.com/coaching.

Studer Group coaches partner with healthcare organizations to create an aligned culture accountable to achieving outcomes together. Working side-by-side, we help to establish, accelerate, and hardwire the necessary changes to create a culture of excellence. This leads to better transparency, higher accountability, and the ability to target and execute specific, objective results that organizations want to achieve.

Studer Group offers coaching based on organizational needs: Evidence-Based Leadership, System Partnership,

Specialized Emergency Department, Huron Physician Solutions, Medical Practice, and Rural Healthcare.

BOOKS: CATEGORIZED BY AUDIENCE

Explore the Fire Starter Publishing website by scanning the QR code with your mobile device or by visiting www.firestarterpublishing.com.

Senior Leaders & Physicians

A Culture of High Performance: Achieving Higher Quality at a Lower Cost—A must-have book for any leader struggling to shore up margins while sustaining an organization that is a great place for employees to work, physicians to practice medicine, and patients to receive care. From best-selling author Quint Studer to help you build a culture that will thrive during change.

Straight A Leadership: Alignment, Action, Accountability—A guide that will help you identify gaps in alignment, action, and accountability; create a plan to fill them; and become a more resourceful, agile, high-performing organization, written by Quint Studer.

Engaging Physicians: A Manual to Physician Partnership—A tactical and passionate road map for physician collaboration to generate organizational high performance, written by Stephen C. Beeson, MD.

Excellence with an Edge: Practicing Medicine in a Competitive Environment—An insightful book that provides practical tools and techniques you need to know to have a solid grasp of the business side of making a living in healthcare, written by Michael T. Harris, MD.

Physicians

Healing Physician Burnout: Diagnosing, Preventing, and Treating— Written by Quint Studer, in collaboration with George Ford, MD, this book helps leaders and physicians work together to create healthy environments for practicing medicine while navigating the huge changes disrupting our industry. It explores why physicians are so burned out and provides practical tools to get them engaged, aligned, and reconnected to their sense of meaning and purpose.

The CG CAHPS Handbook: A Guide to Improve Patient Experience and Clinical Outcomes—Written by Jeff Morris, MD, MBA, FACS; Barbara Hotko, RN, MPA; and Matthew Bates, MPH. *The CG CAHPS Handbook* is your guide for consistently delivering on what matters most to patients and their families and for providing exceptional care and improved clinical outcomes.

Practicing Excellence: A Physician's Manual to Exceptional Health Care—This book, written by Stephen C. Beeson, MD, is a brilliant guide to implementing physician leadership and behaviors that will create a high-performance workplace.

All Leaders

101 Answers to Questions Leaders Ask—By Quint Studer and Studer Group coaches, offers practical, prescriptive solutions from healthcare leaders around the country.

Eat That Cookie!: Make Workplace Positivity Pay Off...For Individuals, Teams, and Organizations—Written by Liz Jazwiec, RN, this book is funny, inspiring, relatable, and is packed with realistic, down-to-earth tactics to infuse positivity into your culture.

Hardwiring Excellence—A *BusinessWeek* bestseller, this book is a road map to creating and sustaining a "Culture of Service and Operational Excellence" that drives bottom-line results. Written by Quint Studer.

Hey Cupcake! We Are ALL Leaders—Author Liz Jazwiec explains that we'll all eventually be called on to lead someone, whether it's a department, a shift, a project team, or a new employee. In her trademark slightly sarcastic (and hilarious) voice, she provides learned-the-hard-way insights that will benefit leaders in every industry and at every level.

"I'm Sorry to Hear That..." Real-Life Responses to Patients' 101 Most Common Complaints About Health Care—When you respond to a patient's complaint, you are responding to the patient's sense of helplessness and anxiety. The service recovery scripts offered in this book can help you recover a patient's confidence in you and your organization. Authored by Susan Keane Baker and Leslie Bank.

Oh No...Not More of That Fluffy Stuff! The Power of Engagement— Written by Rich Bluni, RN, this funny, heartfelt book explores what it takes to overcome obstacles and tap into the passion that fuels our best work. Its practical exercises help employees at all levels get happier, more excited, and more connected to the meaning in our daily lives.

Over Our Heads: An Analogy on Healthcare, Good Intentions, and Unforeseen Consequences— This book, written by Rulon F. Stacey, PhD, FACHE, uses a grocery store analogy to illustrate how government intervention leads to economic crisis and, eventually, collapse.

Results That Last: Hardwiring Behaviors That Will Take Your Company to the Top—A *Wall Street Journal* bestseller by Quint Studer that teaches leaders in every industry how to apply his tactics and strategies to their own organizations to build a corporate culture that consistently reaches and exceeds its goals.

Service Excellence Is As Easy As PIE (Perception Is Everything)—Realistic, down to earth, and wickedly witty, *PIE* is perfect for everyone in healthcare or any other service industry. It's filled with ideas for creating exceptional customer experiences—ideas that are surprising, simple, and yes, easy as you-know-what. Written by Liz Jazwiec.

Taking Conversations from Difficult to Doable—Have you ever dreaded holding a tough but necessary conversation with an employee, coworker, or boss? This book helps you "bite the bullet" and say what needs saying. Learn tools and tactics to navigate tough conversations confidently and effectively. Written by Lynne Cunningham.

The Great Employee Handbook: Making Work and Life Better—This book is a valuable resource for employees at all levels who want to learn how to handle tough workplace situations—skills that normally come only from a lifetime of experience. *Wall Street Journal* best-selling author Quint Studer has pulled together the best insights gained from working with thousands of employees during his career.

Nurse Leaders and Nurses

Inspired Nurse and *Inspired Journal*—By Rich Bluni, RN, help maintain and recapture the inspiration nurses felt at the start of their journey with action-oriented "spiritual stretches" and stories that illuminate those sacred moments we all experience.

Inspired Nurse Too—The follow up to Rich Bluni, RN's, best-seller and award-winning *Inspired Nurse, Inspired Nurse Too* will make you laugh, cry, reconnect to your sense of meaning and purpose, and remember to be grateful for the incredible work you do every day. Most of all, it will help you sustain the energy and passion you need to provide the extraordinary care your patients need, expect, and deserve.

The HCAHPS Handbook, 2nd Edition: Tactics to Improve Quality and the Patient Experience—Revised and released in 2015, this book is a valuable resource for organizations seeking to provide the exceptional quality of care their patients expect and deserve. Coauthored by Lyn Ketelsen, RN, MBA; Karen Cook, RN; and Bekki Kennedy.

The Nurse Leader Handbook: The Art and Science of Nurse Leadership—By Studer Group senior nursing and physician leaders from across the country, is filled with knowledge that provides nurse leaders with a solid foundation for success. It also serves as a reference they can revisit again and again when they have questions or need a quick refresher course in a particular area of the job.

Emergency Department Team

Advance Your Emergency Department: Leading in a New Era—As this critical book asserts, world-class Emergency Departments don't follow. They lead. Stephanie J. Baker, RN, CEN, MBA; Regina Shupe, RN, MSN, CEN; and Dan Smith, MD, FACEP, share high-impact strategies and tactics to help your ED get results more efficiently, effectively, and collaboratively. Master them and you'll improve quality, exceed patient expectations, and ultimately help the entire organization maintain and grow its profit margin.

Excellence in the Emergency Department: How to Get Results—A book by Stephanie Baker, RN, CEN, MBA, is filled with proven, easy-to-implement, step-by-step instructions that will help you move your Emergency Department forward.

Hardwiring Flow: Systems and Processes for Seamless Patient Care—Drs. Thom Mayer and Kirk Jensen delve into one of the most critical issues facing healthcare leaders: patient flow.

The Patient Flow Advantage: How Hardwiring Hospital-Wide Flow Drives Competitive Performance—Build effectiveness, efficiency, and a patient-centric focus into the heart of every process that serves the patient. Efficient patient flow has never been more critical to ensure patient safety, satisfaction, and optimal reimbursement. Authored by Drs. Kirk Jensen and Thom Mayer.

STUDER CONFERENCES:

Learn more about Studer Group conferences by scanning the QR code with your mobile device or by visiting www.studergroup.com/conferences.

Studer Conferences are three-day interactive learning events designed to provide healthcare leaders with an authentic, practical learning experience. Each Studer Conference includes internationally renowned keynote speakers and tracks concentrated on key areas of the healthcare organization. Every track includes breakout sessions and "how-to" workshops that provide you with direct access to experts and conference faculty. The faculty at Studer Conferences go beyond PowerPoint slides and lectures to show you "what right looks like."

Leaders will leave with new tools and skills that get results. Find out more about upcoming Studer Conferences and register at www.studergroup.com/conferences.

All Studer Group Conferences offer Continuing Education Credits. For more information on CMEs, visit www.studergroup.com/cmecredits.

STUDER SPEAKING:

Learn more about Studer Group speaking by scanning the QR code with your mobile device or by visiting www.studergroup.com/speaking.

From large association events to exclusive executive training, Studer Group speakers deliver the perfect balance of inspiration and education for every audience. As experienced clinicians and administrators, each speaker has a unique journey to share. This personal touch along with hard-hitting healthcare improvement tactics empower your team to take action and drive organizational growth with training that reaches leaders at all levels.

Additional Books by Jacquelyn Gaines

The Yellow Suit: A Guide for Women in Leadership—
This book includes all those things women usually share with each other in private, those things we wish someone had told us about being a leader—unvarnished truths. In it, Jackie provides steps women must take if they want to become effective leaders in today's workforce, emphasizes the importance of women taking control of their careers, and shows them how to do it. Packed with enlightened insights, helpful anecdotes, and practical tools, the book examines the unique challenges that leadership presents and focuses on professional and personal development.

Believing You Can Fly—Jacquelyn Gaines joined the workforce as a nurse. Her dedication and compassion made her a favorite among her patients, but her superiors weren't always so impressed. This is the true story of a woman who turned her dream of helping people into a rewarding 30-year career in healthcare. This inspiring book shares one woman's experiences in the healthcare field, as she overcame prejudice to excel in her career.

Destination Infinity: Reflections and Career Lessons from a Road Warrior—Using the experiences of those who regularly travel for work, this book offers career lessons found along the journey by "road warriors." Many may give you pause about your own career, and some are life parodies that will make you smile. In the end, you will see that there are no limits to where you can go if you leave the door open to the possibilities.

About the Author

Jackie Gaines is a high-performing senior executive with a progressive career encompassing more than 38 years of sustained leadership and accomplishments with major health systems and organizations. With passion, creative energy, and vision, she motivates diverse groups of people toward success. She has dedicated most of her career to the advancement of quality  healthcare programs throughout the United States, particularly those focused on the care of the poor and underserved. She has worked in a variety of roles, starting her career as a nurse working for Johns Hopkins Health Institutions, including management, health education, and program coordination. Upon graduation from her master's program, she went to work for Health Care for the Homeless, Inc., in Baltimore,

Maryland, as a nurse practitioner serving over 50,000 vulnerable patients per year in clinics, shelters, and the streets. In 1987, she was appointed as its first president and CEO and developed this organization into a national model.

In 1999, Jackie was appointed vice president of community health systems integration for Bon Secours Baltimore Health System. There Jackie led an effective $15 million turnaround initiative called Transformation 2000. In 2000 Jackie joined the Providence Health System in Oregon as chief executive for Providence Milwaukie Hospital and regional chief executive for ancillary business. While at Providence, Jackie took Providence Milwaukie to the Top 100 Hospitals in the U.S. list three times and implemented the organization's Family Practice Residency Program. In 2007 Jackie left Providence to become the president and CEO of Mercy Health Partners for Northeast Pennsylvania, where she had oversight of two hospitals and 15 other freestanding clinics and diagnostic centers.

Jackie lectures all over the country and has received numerous awards along the way. She has written four books, *Wait a Hot Minute! How to Manage Your Life with the Minutes You Have*, *Believing You Can Fly*, *The Yellow Suit: A Guide for Women in Leadership*, and *Destination Infinity: Reflections and Career Lessons from a Road Warrior*. Today, Jackie is an executive coach for Studer Group®, a Huron Healthcare solution. She lives in North Carolina with her husband, Wesley, enjoying the beauty and rich culture of the area and their three grandchildren. She also is a licensed ZIN Zumba instructor.

How to Order Additional Copies of

Wait a Hot Minute!

Orders may be placed:

Online at:
www.firestarterpublishing.com/wait-a-hot-minute

Scan the QR code with your mobile device to order through the Fire
Starter Publishing website.

By phone at: 866-354-3473

By mail at: Fire Starter Publishing
350 W. Cedar Street, Suite 300
Pensacola, FL 32502

Share this book with your team—and save!
Wait a Hot Minute! is filled with inspirational and practical information.
If purchasing for a team to share, please contact Fire Starter Publishing
at 866-354-3473 to learn more about volume savings.